FLY FLYER FLY

Louis Bou

monsa

CLUB 13
PINK FLAMINGO
Bongo Lounge
agosto 04
discount 3€

BARCELONA
MUSIC
SUNDAYS
PIN-UP'S
candy candy nights
3.10.03
80's
babies are
electro!
lady Miss Kier
Deee Lites
and
Eva
viernes 30 de abril

Fly Flyer Fly

Editor
Josep Mª Minguet

Autor
Texto, diseño y fotografías
Text, design and photographs
Louis Bou Romero
Equipo editorial Monsa

Gravina 43 (08930)
Sant Adrià de Besòs
Barcelona
Tlf. +34 93 381 00 50
Fax. +34 93 381 00 93
www.monsa.com
monsa@monsa.com

ISBN 84-96429-23-7
D.L B-7.096-2006

Printed by
Impreso por
Industrias Gráficas Mármol

CONTENTS

WHERE'S THE PARTY?	**six**
¿Dónde está la fiesta?	seis
DESIGN...NO RULES!	**eight**
Diseña...¡Sin reglas!	ocho
GIVING IT PROPS	**twenty four**
Formas y materiales	veinticuatro
LOGOS + TYPES	**fifty four**
Logos + Tipografías	cicuenta y cuatro
POSTERS	**ninety eight**
Pósters	noventa y ocho
FREAK	**one hundred and thirty**
Freak, trash, bizzarre, kistch	ciento treinta
SEX PORNOCHIC	**one hundred and sixty four**
Sexo	ciento sesenta y cuatro
RETRO	**one hundred and ninety**
Regreso al pasado	ciento noventa
FLYERS FLYERS FLYERS	**two hundred and six**
	doscientos seis

CONTENIDO

DISCOTHÈQUE
pin up's
WINTER'03 · ESTACIÓN DE FRANCIA
www.tonfone.com
SALSITAS
Sin Flyer 20 €
discothequebcn.com

INTRO

WHERE'S THE PARTY?

¿Dónde está la fiesta?

Una noche cualquiera en una ciudad cualquiera millones de jóvenes de todo el mundo tienen como común denominador la misma pregunta: "¿A que discoteca vamos a ir esta noche?"... Por suerte siempre alguien saca un flyer arrugado del fondo de algún bolsillo solucionando el "grave" problema.
En un flyer encontramos toda la información que necesitamos saber: dirección del club, el Dj que pincha esa noche, precios y descuentos, y como no, hasta el modo en que tenemos que ir vestidos. El lenguaje tiene que ser claro y el mensaje visual directo, cuanto más impactante y vistoso sea el diseño del flyer más poder de atracción ejercerá entre el público. El flyer es la imagen del club, la muestra efímera de lo que nos esperará cuando crucemos la puerta de la discoteca y hallamos pagado nuestra entrada. Como estandarte de la imagen del club, el diseño del flyer define a la perfección lo que vamos a encontrar al llegar allí, por lo que en pocos casos las sorpresas o decepciones están garantizadas. Así como los distintos estilos de música, pop, rock, heavy metal tienen un lenguaje visual específico, el diseño del flyer para la música de baile tiene también su propio estilo que va cambiando al ritmo que cambian las modas y la cultura. Sin flyer no hay fiesta y sin fiesta no hay club. Cualquier club que se precie destina parte del presupuesto semanal a la promoción del local y de sus fiestas, por lo tanto como mínimo divulga uno o más flyers semanales por toda la ciudad: en bares, tiendas de ropa y demás locales diurnos y nocturnos de moda, frecuentados en su mayoría por un público joven ávido de pasarlo bien, bailando hasta altas horas de la madrugada. La promoción y una buena distribución facilitan muchísimo la labor de búsqueda a aquellos recién llegados a una ciudad en busca del mejor club o del local de moda.
Este libro nos invita a un viaje a través del apasionante y divertido mundo de la cultura club representada gráficamente por flyers de diferentes partes del mundo.
El flyer es el pasaporte de los "clubbers" hacia la diversión...
¡sin flyer estarían perdidos!

A night on the town in any city and millions of young people the world over will be asking the same question: "So where's the party?"... Sure enough there's always someone who pulls a crumpled flyer from the depths of their back pocket to solve the "serious" problem.
The flyer tells us all we need to know: the location of the club, which DJ is on tonight, prices, discounts, even the way we are expected to dress. The message has to be clear and the visual communication direct, the more eye-catching is the flyer, the more likely it is to make an impact on the public. The flyer represents the club's identity, a fleeting glimpse of what awaits us once we cross the threshold and find ourselves paying the discotheque entrance fee. Like a banner sporting the image of the club, the flyer defines to perfection exactly what we can expect to find on our arrival, guaranteeing no nasty surprises or disappointments. Just as different kinds of music, whether pop, rock or heavy metal, have their own specific visual language, flyers for dance music also have a design of their own continuously being transformed at a pace akin to that of the latest fashions and cultures.
Without the flyer there's no party and without the party there's no club. Any self-respecting club sets aside part of the weekly budget to promote both the place itself and its forthcoming events, at the very least by distributing one or two flyers a week across the city: in bars, fashion shops and other fashionable daytime hangouts and night time haunts which are frequented mainly by a young clientele intent on having a good time, dancing until the early hours. Good, efficiently distributed advertising makes it all the more easy for those new to the city looking for the best club or the trendiest place.
This book takes us on a journey through the fascinating and entertaining world of the culture club, graphically represented by flyers from around the world.
The flyer is the "clubbers" passport to a good time...
without the flyer they are lost!

CARN
(AVAL)
PIRATAS
DJ TANIA VULCANO
1 SÁBADO MARZO
discothèque
barcelona
EVERY FRIDAY AND SATURDAY FROM MIDNIGHT TILL MORNING VIP RESERVATIONS 638 222 891 · CLUB & PRESS INFOLINE: 93 272 49 80
BARCELONA'S MOST FABULOUS NIGHT CLUB
LUCKY STRIKE

En estas páginas / On these pages
Discothèque I Barcelona I Toni Colomar
Nightsun Group I Barcelona I Toni Colomar

Diseña...¡Sin reglas!

El diseño de flyers no tiene fronteras, el creador tiene absoluta potestad para diseñarlo por lo que podemos encontrarnos con todo tipo de colores, formas, texturas y materiales.
El flyer como actualmente se le conoce nace en los ochenta y arrasa en grandes ciudades como Nueva York o Londres. Las tiendas de música, moda, y bares más frecuentadas por el público en general, se llenaban de flyers cumpliendo su función informativa. Su creación y materiales eran básicos, es decir, papel tipo folio y fotocopias en blanco y negro, en raras ocasiones coloreados a mano, ya que el presupuesto no permitía las cuatricomías, plastificados, troqueles y sofisticaciones a las que estamos acostumbrados hoy en día. La infraestructura era muy pequeña y el presupuesto que se necesitaba era impensable, por ejemplo el precio de la impresión llegaba a ser diez veces superior de lo que cuesta hoy. A mediados de los años noventa, la era digital trajo una herramienta indispensable hoy en día para todo diseñador gráfico: el ordenador personal. El ordenador aporta todas las herramientas de diseño necesarias en una: tratamiento de imágenes, creación de textos y tipografías, maquetación, dibujo vectorial, etc...
Es entonces cuando todos los clubs y discotecas comenzaron a hacer sus flyers, una manera de llegar al gran público con un bajo presupuesto sin tener que gastar fortunas en otro tipo de publicidad. Jóvenes diseñadores de todo el mundo aprendieron a utilizar la preciada herramienta digital que les permitía dar rienda suelta a su imaginación. No solo ahorraba tiempo sino que se podían conseguir efectos y montajes imposibles de realizar a mano. Nace pues un nuevo medio de expresión donde lo que cuenta es la provocación visual y la originalidad.

The design of flyers comes with neither rules nor regulations, the creator having absolute power and the reason for which we encounter all manner of colours, shapes, textures and materials.
The flyer as we know it is a product of the eighties, hugely successful in big cities the likes of New York and London. Music stores, trendy bars and shops most frequented by the general public were inundated with flyers carrying out their informative role. Their creation and material were at the time fairly basic, that is to say, a sheet of paper photocopied in black and white, on rare occasions coloured by hand, especially since the budget at that time would have permitted the four-colour processes, plastic coating, die cutting and sophistications we are accustomed to nowadays. The infrastructure was at the time minute and the required budget unthinkable, the price of printing was for example ten times what it costs today. In the mid nineties, the digital era brought with it an indispensable modern tool for designers in the field of graphic arts: the personal computer. The computer provided all the necessary design tools in one, for the processing of images, the creation of texts and typography, page layouts, vectorial sketches, etc...
It was then when the all the clubs and discotheques began to make their own flyers as a means of reaching the public without having to spend a fortune on other forms of publicity. Young designers the world over learnt to use the valuable tool which allowed them to give free reign to their imagination. Not only did they save time but they were able to achieve effects and montages which were impossible by hand. A new form of expression was born in which the central theme was visual provocation and originality.

domingo 06.04.2003 desde 19:00
tribute to ibiza
DJ' JONATHAN ULYSSES (Space Ibiza) - DJ' GEE (Bora-Bora)
DJ' CESAR DEL RIO (Privilege) - DJ' OLIVER (Amnesia)
artista invitada: GLAMOUR TO KILL (Decadence)
MATINEE

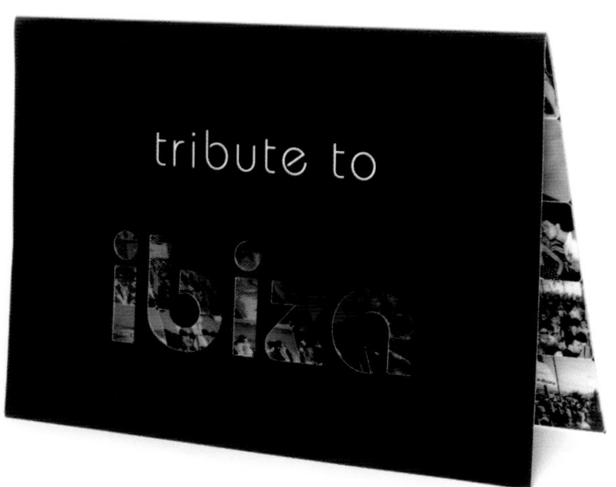
tribute to
ibiza

FLORIDA
www.florida135.com
135

FLORIDA
www.florida135.com
135

club
danzatoria

BILLY BOY
GAY DISCO
BCN
GAY DISCO

Página izquierda / Left page
Matineé Group | Barcelona | Neus Cardona
Florida 135 | Huesca | Charly Brown
Club Danzatoria | Barcelona | clubcatwalk.net
Billy Boy | Barcelona
En esta página / This page
Club Danzatoria | Barcelona | clubcatwalk.net

The 1st Friday of every Month
ISSUED BY PACHA LONDON Airlines

FRIDAY 4th JUNE 2004

GATE 21
PACHA LONDON * TERMINUS PLACE SW1 * TELEPHONE: 020 7833 3139
NOT VALID FOR
TRANSPORTATION
FROM NEW YORK (USA) TO LONDON (UK)

DECK CAPTAINS (TERMINAL 1) ZT 5F65 E/ 1AW
FULL INTENTION SCOTT CUBA GREG MAY
PAV (Europes finest percussionist)
INSPIRIT MUSIC FLIGHT ATTENDANTS (TERMINAL 2)
The Beard Amma (Live PA) West of Centre

ADMISSION
GBP £15 £12 B4 11.30
CONCESSIONS
GBP £10 CALL 020 7833 3139
scott@pachalondon.com
07956 480473

T 25 554 000 6566
04545465500 40

Boarding Pass
GATE 21

DRESS
"LONDON CALLING"
SUPERGLAM & STYLISH

CARRIER/FLIGHT		CLASS/DATE	TIME
PACHA		TBA	TBA
GATE	BOARD TIME	SEAT	SMOKE
21	22.00 / 04.00	FIRST CLASS	*

FROM NEW YORK (USA) TO LONDON (UK)
NOT VALID FOR TRAVEL
0 5235111866 75 65445 8

Valentine's Day
February 14, 2003
discount
Valentine's Day
February 14, 2003
Share Your Love With Us
Valentine's Day · February 14, 2003
DJ Lofty
(Chili Funk Records) · UK
Dr. Pepe
Tomas Boo
Starts at 21.00
WWW.CLUBGRAVITY.LT

MONTJUÏC

MONTJUÏC

FANCY
FLY
ME!
727
INTERNATIONAL
KEN

En estas páginas / These pages
Club Gravity I Vilnius, Lithuania I clubgravity.lt

dancing globe
Dancing Globe
March 13
Saturday 22:00
LENNY FONTANA (NY)
www.clubgravity.lt

Mr C.
(THE SHAMEN, UK)
Tadeu Nice
(Deep Inc., LT)
DANCING GLOBE #6
dancing globe
Mr C.
(THE SHAMEN, UK)
Tadeu Nice
(Deep Inc., LT)
DANCING GLOBE #6
May 15 Saturday 22:00
www.clubgravity.lt
Club Gravity · Jasinskio str. 16, LT-2001 Vilnius, Lithuania
Entrance from Geležinis Vilkas street / Tel +370 5 2497966
info@clubgravity.lt

Ian Pooley
(Germany)
Tadeu Nice (Deep Inc., LT)
www.clubgravity.lt
DANCING GLOBE #5
May 17 Saturday 22:00
DANCING GLOBE #5
Gravity

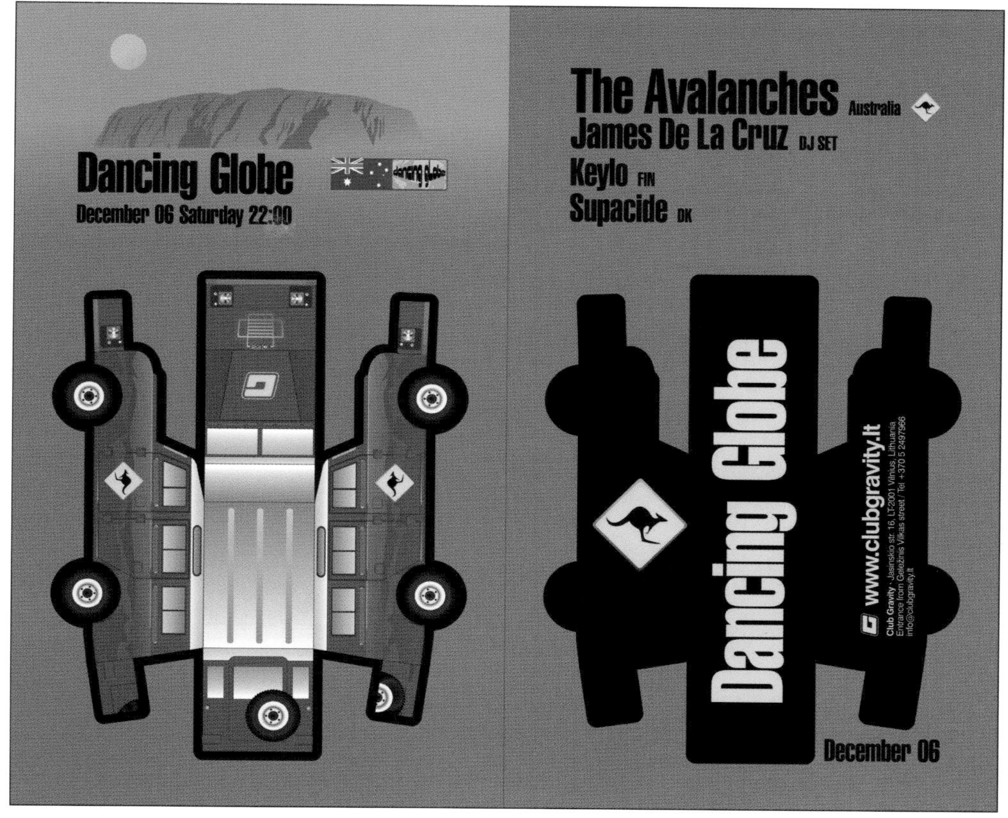
Dancing Globe
December 06 Saturday 22:00
The Avalanches Australia
James De La Cruz DJ SET
Keylo FIN
Supacide DK
Dancing Globe
www.clubgravity.lt
December 06

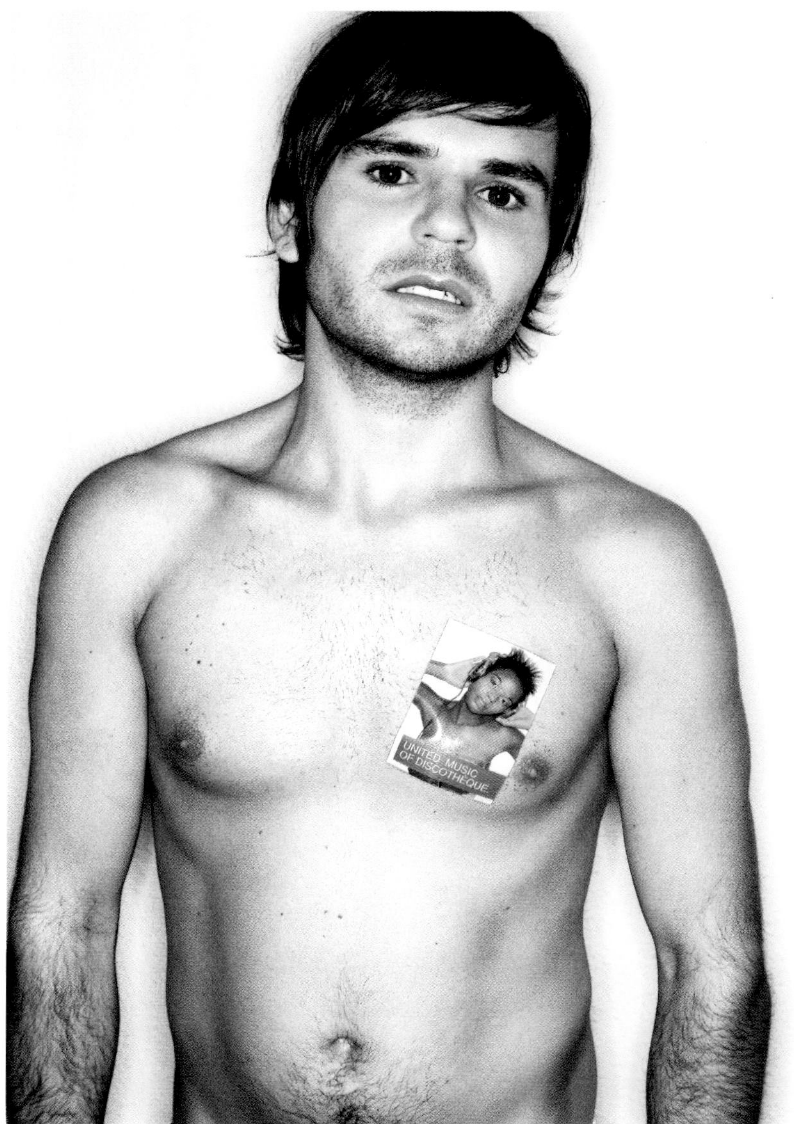

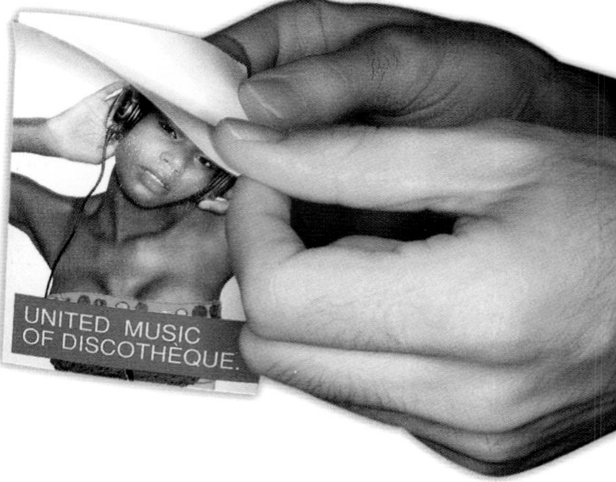

UNITED MUSIC
OF DISCOTHÈQUE.

viernes 17
de septiembre
OPENING
NEW SEASON
AUTUMN / WINTER
2004/2005
con vinny da vinci (sudáfrica)
matt caselli (ibiza), lee stark (barcelona)
jekey (hip-hop set), live de luca g. plus
50 dancing divas... y tu
PEGATE EL ADHESIVO EN EL CORAZÓN
Y SI ENTREGAS ESTE DORSO EN LA
PUERTA ANTES DE LAS 2 H. ENTRAS
GRATIS Y TE INVITAMOS A UNA COPA
condicionado al aforo y normas de acceso al local

SALVATION
1
ANIVERSARIO
JUEVES
18 DE MAYO DEL 2000
24:00H.

1
ANIVERSARIO
SALVATION
GAY DISCO
MATINEE GROUP AGRADECE EL APOYO DE TODOS LOS COLABORADORES
Y CLIENTES, QUE HAN HECHO POSIBLE DURANTE 365 DIAS DE SALVATION
UNA SALA PARA ESTAR APARTE SIN SER DIFERENTES.

1
ANIVERSARIO
SALVATION
GAY DISCO
MATINEE GROUP AGRADECE EL APOYO DE TODOS LOS COLABORADORES
Y CLIENTES, QUE HAN HECHO POSIBLE DURANTE 365 DIAS DE SALVATION
UNA SALA PARA ESTAR APARTE SIN SER DIFERENTES.

BOUDOIR
Join us on the biggest night of the year as Café dresses itself to the nines in homage to the loudest, bravest, longest party in history. The Berlin Burlesque shows screamed onto the scene in 1901 and roared for over thirty years until the doors were nailed shut by the authorities in '33.
Expect the most jaw-droppingly outrageous stage acts ever seen. Expect the very finest DJs putting needle to vinyl including Paul Harris of Dirty Vegas and our erstwhile residents, T-Money and Matt Harris. Expect towering stilt walkers and angelic divas. Expect to be pampered at every turn. Expect a very, very special guest and expect it to run and run and run.
Burn your diary. Trash your PDA. Rip up the TV listings and forget Auld Lang Syne. Smile as we take you by the hand and take you back to a time when live cabaret was dangerous and dark and a world away from your normal lives.
Doors: 6pm – 6am
Champagne and Canape Reception: 9-10 pm
Cabaret and DJs to run until they drop
Limited Discount Tickets @ £40 until 1st December 2003. £60 thereafter.
Three course restaurant and club ticket £99.
Enquiries/Restaurant/Drinking Tables:
020 7395 5806
Email: tickets@cafedeparis.com
New Year's Eve @ Café - Do not miss it.
Paris
New Year's Eve@
ELECTRIC BERLIN
BOUDOIR

Discothèque | Barcelona | Toni Colomar

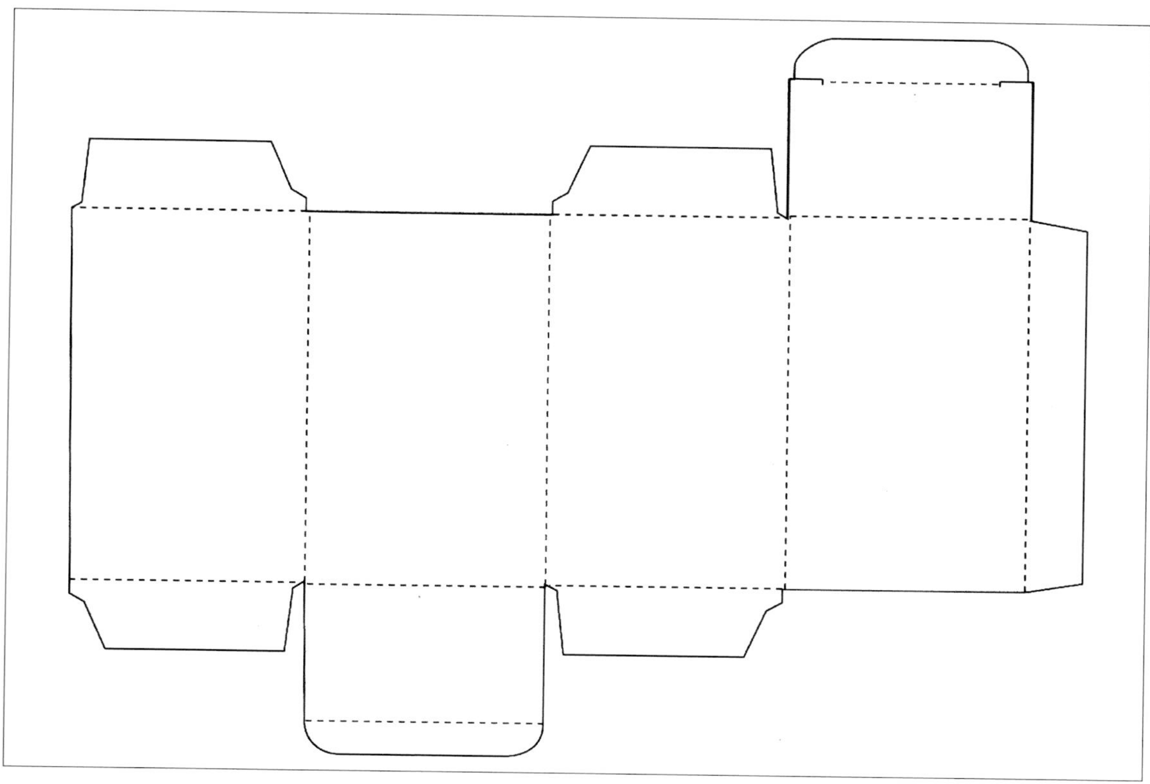

de
LUCA G
fragance
· spray de musique ·
· natural de discothèque ·
· vaporisateur ·
27nov2004
100ml
DIS
COTH
EQUE
D
CLUB
abierto viernes sábados y vísperas.
precio de la botella y mesa:150 euros
reservas de mesas vip: 636 222 891
otras infos: 93 511 57 64
subscribe to www.helice.info
art work by www.tonicolomar.com
de
LUCA G
fragance
· sábado 27 noviembre 04 ·
let yourself got sprayed
by dj Lee Stark
hosting the show
Luca G
In The Black Room
dj miss shampoo
LUCKY STRIKE
3 EUROS DE DESCUENTO
CON ESTE FLYER A CUALQUIER HORA
D

En esta página / This page
Pacha I Barcelona I clubpachabcn.com
Acapulco I Zurich I Nadine Geissbühler
Página derecha / Right page
Club Mascotte I Zurich I Nadine Geissbühler

Bis Ende August bleibt das Mascotte am Montag, Dienstag, Mittwoch und Sonntag geschlossen. Ab September geht's dann mit vollem Programm wieder los. Wir freuen uns schon drauf!
JEDEN DONNERSTAG AB 23.00
Silk
This is my Night
DJS STYLEBOX 1658 AND DJ TEAM
Silk ONE YEAR BIRTHDAY-NIGHT!
MAXIMO PARK
The First Lady
Silk AALIYAH SPECIAL
JEDEN FREITAG AB 23.00
DJS DON ALFONZO & FRÄNE
DJS MURI & UJO
DJS PROMILLO & FRÄNE
DJS MURI & GRAU
SAMSTAG
the message
LIPSTICK
MORPH
VORSCHAU
8.9.2005
KARAOKE FROM HELL
"SEASON KICK OFF"
10.9.2005
LAITH AL-DEEN (D)
23.9.2005
BLACKMAIL (D)
www.blackmail-music.com
15.&16.10.2005
GABBA GABBA HEY!
DAS RAMONES-MUSICAL
www.gabbagabbahey.info
11.11.2005
VIVE LA FÊTE (B)
www.vivelafete.net
HAPPY BIRTHDAY
MASCOTTE
1 YEAR
CORSO
JANUAR 2005
APERO: DIENSTAG BIS FREITAG AB 17.00
APRIL 2005
O: DIENSTAG BIS FREITAG AB 17.00
BELLEVUE ZÜRICH WWW.MASCOTTE.CH
NOVEMBER 2004
MONTAG BIS FREITAG AB 17.00
VORSCHAU
FERRIS MC & DJ STYLEWARZ
mascotte
JUNI 2005
DEZEMBER
APERO: MONTAG BIS FR
MONTAG GESCHLOSSEN
DIENSTAG
KARAOKE FROM HELL
THE BOYS ARE BACK IN TOWN... MIT VIELEN NEUEN SONGS

NEW!
FRESH AIR FROM PARIS!
I ♥ PARIS
LA TOUR EIFFEL
I Paris

GIVING IT PROPS!

Shape+Size+Materials

Formas+materiales

El flyer tiene que llamar la atención del cliente, es la imagen de la empresa que se vende, es la tarjeta de presentación y definirá a que tipo de público está destinado.
El flyer evoluciona rápidamente, no sólo tecnológicamente, sino que se adapta rápidamente a los nuevos ritmos que marcan la moda y el arte. Los diseñadores experimentan, evolucionan y crean nuevas tendencias logrando sintetizar el mensaje o significado del flyer en una sola imagen.
Aunque su elaboración pasando desde el primer concepto o boceto hasta su llegada a las calles es muy laboriosa, el flyer es sobre todo un lenguaje artístico efímero, tiene una vida muy corta, ya que su cometido informativo dura una o dos semanas y luego termina en el cubo de la basura, también puede suceder que llegue a formar parte de la colección privada de algún joven o diseñador que lo inmortalice pegado con una chincheta a la pared de su habitación junto con los pósters de sus artistas favoritos.
El flyer como medio de comunicación sólo podrá verse afectado cuando las nuevas tecnologías como internet lo sustituyan por e-mails o mensajes a teléfonos móviles. Muchos clubs ya ofrecen la posibilidad de conectarse a su web y descargar "e-flyers", que después de ser impresos en nuestra casa con una impresora doméstica serán canjeados por descuentos o invitaciones al llegar a la puerta del club.

The flyer aims to draw the client's attention, it represents the image of the company who is selling it, the presentation card, also defining to which sector of the public it is aimed at.
The flyer has evolved very rapidly, not only technologically speaking, but by adapting and keeping pace with art and fashion. Designers experiment, develop and create new trends finally synthesising the flyer's message or meaning into a single image.
The production process from the time of the initial idea or outline until reaching the streets is quite laborious, the flyer being above all an ephemeral short-lived artistic representation with an informative mission lasting only one or two weeks, ending up in the rubbish bin, but that said, it might also form a part of some youngster's or designer's private collection, anchored to the bedroom wall by a drawing pin to be immortalised alongside posters of their favourite singers and artists.
The flyer as a means of communication will only be affected when the new technologies such as internet replace it by e-mails or mobile phone messages. Many clubs already provide web sites to connect and download "e-flyers" which after being printed at home on the household printer can be exchanged for discounts or passes at the club door.

Discothèque | Barcelona | Crazybabyl

ILUSTRACION:WWW.IVANSOLDO.COM
SAY WHAT
PARTY PEOPLE
DISCO KING
Ilustracion: www.ivansoldo.com

Rocking
Birthday
Discothèque
7 years

VIERNES
15 OCTUBRE 2004
SUPER GUEST DJ
MARTIN SOLVEIG
WARM UP LEE STARK
IN THE BLACK ROOM JEKEY (HIP HOP SET)
7º ANIVERSARIO
DIS
COTH
ÈQUE
D
CLUB
ABIERTO VIERNES SÁBADOS Y VÍSPERAS PRECIO DE LA BOTELLA Y MESA: 150 EUROS. RESERVAS DE MESAS VIP: 636 222 891.. OTRAS INFOS: 93 511 57 64. POBLE ESPANYOL MONTJUÏC. BARCELONA'S MOST FABULOUS NIGHT CLUB. WWW.HELICE.INFO

Club Mascotte | Zurich | Nadine Geissbühler

De arriba a abajo / From top left to right
Mondo @ Stella | Madrid
The Room @ Stella | Madrid
The Room @ Stella | Madrid
New York Club | Barcelona
Bongo Lounge @ La Paloma | Barcelona | Mariana Sarraute
The Room The Room @ Stella | Madrid
Discothèque | Barcelona | Toni Colomar
Club Mascotte | Zurich | Nadine Geissbühler

Desembre 2002

5. ALBERT MIRANDA (SANAE GROUP/GI)
6. PLACID (WWW.ACID-HOUSE.NET/LONDON)
ANDREAS (WWW.LAESK.COM/BCN)
7. RON´S MOBILE DISCO (ONE LOUDER/DUBLIN)
14. 1er Anniversari de "REBELTECH DJS"
MARK BROOM (PUREPLASTIC/LONDON)
JAVIER ORDUÑA (REBELTECH/BCN)
BRUCE LEE (REBELTECH/BCN)
21. AN DER BEAT live act (MINIFUNK/PLF)
24. MARTIAN (WWW.MARTIAN.COM)
25. MARKX (INFERSOUND/VIC)
28. ROBERT X (MOOG/BCN)

31. Cap d'any 2003. Nuit de Saint-Sylvestre.
Sala 1 (techno). KARZ & NONE live act (GI)
MARIO RIVEIRO (BCN)
Sala 2 (house). ROBIN BALL (GROOVEPLEASURE/LONDON)
ESTEBAN (ENJOY REC./ CÉRET)
Sala 3 (DRUM&BASS). RANDOM + DRESDEN CODEX (ASYNCHRONE/PARIS)

Gener 2003

4. JROB (MULTIDIMENSIONAL/TOULOUSE)
5. LOKI (PARADISE FORWARD/GI)

Djs residents: DJOSEP/MATT/PHERE

La discoteca "Le Rachdingue" romandrà tancada per vacances els caps de setmana dels 12, 19 i 26 de gener.
La discothèque "Le Rachdingue" sera en vacances les week-ends du 12, 19 et 26 janvier.

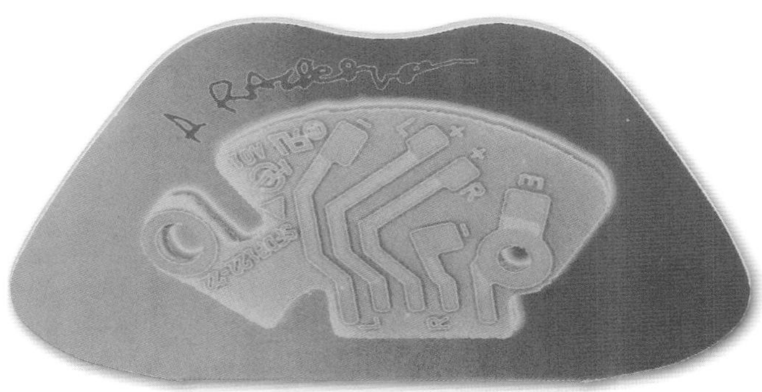

Le Rachdingue | Gerona | Ivan

La Madame | Barcelona | Neus Cardona

CRIMEN
in club
danzatoria
MARINA VILLAGE
RAMON TRIAS FARGAS S/N
DESIGN BY R.RENAN
viernes
24/01/03
CRIMEN
IN club
Freday
danzatoria
MARINA VILLAGE
RAMOM TRIAS FARGAS S/N
CRIMEN Producciones & M.A.R.C
Toni Bass
CRIMEN
in club
CRIMEN
in club
danzatoria

La Suite
27 club
www.lasuite27.com
Open everynight from 23.30 h.

La Suite
27
INAUGURACION
viernes 30 de abril

Fantasti-Ka
VIERNES NOCHE
FRIDAY NIGHT
26
AGOSTO
AUGUST
space
DANCE BARCELONA

Fantasti-Ka
space
DANCE BARCELONA
VIERNES NOCHE
FRIDAY NIGHT
26
NOVIEMBRE
NOVEMBER

Fantasti-Ka
space
DANCE BARCELONA
VIERNES NOCHE
FRIDAY NIGHT
22
ABRIL
APRIL

Fantasti-Ka
VIERNES NOCHE
FRIDAY NIGHT
08
OCTUBRE
OCTOBER
space
DANCE BARCELONA

HAPPY NEW YEAR
SALVATION
Gay Disco
31 de diciembre de 2002
GO TO THE CLUB
...LAS VEGAS
PARK
SUITE

Lokotron I Barcelona I lokotron.com
La Sal bcn I Barcelona I sitosdf.com
The Joint I London I adamation.co.uk

Pacha Barcelona | Barcelona | clubpachabcn.com
Café Olé | Ibiza | Neus Cardona
Devotion | San Francisco | theendup.com
Emotion | Madrid
La Atlàntida | Barcelona | latlantida.com
Café de Paris | London | cafedeparis.com

Zouk Club | Singapore | Jimmy

Club Mascotte | Zurich | Nadine Geissbühler
Zouk Club | Singapore | Jimmy

RESIDENT DJS UJO, DON ALFONZO, MURI, GRAU, P.A.T., TOM FRIDAY, PITSCH
POP · ROCK · 80'S · DISCO · WAVE · NDW · HIP HOP · RNB · REGGAE · RAGGA · OLDIES · NEWS
ALL STYLES - ALL STARS
the Royal Flush
Shake your Ace!
JEDEN FREITAG AB 23 UHR
BELLEVUE ✦ MASCOTTE ✦ ZÜRICH

NEWSLETTER: WWW.MASCOTTE.CH

NEWSLETTER: WWW.MASCOTTE.CH

NEWSLETTER: WWW.MASCOTTE.CH

Salón de los Espejos
Set Live – House minimal
Hospital :: Nol.cometa
(Live) Dpendiente Colectivo (Chile-BCN) (Set)
Elástico (Poker Club)
Punkdongo Music Recordings
The Bad Room
elektro house
Fernanda Díaz (Poker Club)
Art Mago Julián
Produced by Provoca Jaime
3€
PRE-PARTY Daf Art&Club
23h. - ALTAS ESFERAS (Live)
SEA KEY (San Pol de mar)
Plaça dels Angels 5-6
Domingo 5 de Junio, 17h. • Poker Beach • San Pol de mar
CLUB FELLINI • POKER CLUB • LAS RAMBLAS 27
open from monday to saturday from 23h.
www.nightsungroup.com www.clubfellini.com

02-06-05
Poker Club
JUEVES
2
JUNIO
Club Fellini

POKER CLUB
JUEVES
10
MARZO
2005
CLUB FELLINI

El Salón de los Espejos
Music definition?
VINCENZO (Dessous)
Elástico (Daf)
JUEVES
10
MARZO
The Bad Room
Music definition?
Fernanda Díaz
(www.fernandadíaz.com)
ScannerFM.com
3€
Art
MagoJulián (Salón Magico-Tigre 10)
Myfancymanfrancis (Visuals)
Produced by Provoca Jaime
Colaboran
TRAX-Música electrónica & clubbing
ScannerFM.com
Daf Art&Club
CLUB FELLIBI • POKER CLUB • LAS RAMBLAS 27
Open on Thursdays, Fridays, Saturdays & before holidays fromm 00h.
www.clubfellini.com

Not
@ZOUK
ZOUK

Not
@
ZOUK
ZOUK

Not @ ZOUK
ZOUK™

VIERNES 6 JUNIO
CRIMEN 08
by M.A.R.C.
Ego & Babe
EGOIST & BABY FACE
ELECTRO FETISH EXPERIENCE
& the residents
PRE PARTY
SALSITAS
danzatoria
TIBIDABO
Jordi Goberna • Javier Naviné
fashion live:
HYBRID
by Manuel Albarrán
Slider at work & video: Solly & Fausto
ArtWork
R.Renan y Oskr
agradecimientos
www.clear-bcn.com
club
danzatoria
Marina Villa
Ramón Tria
Fargas s/
BARCELONA

Club Danzatoria | Barcelona | R.Renan & Oskr

Club Danzatoria | Barcelona | clubcatwalk.net
Shôko | Barcelona | shoko.biz

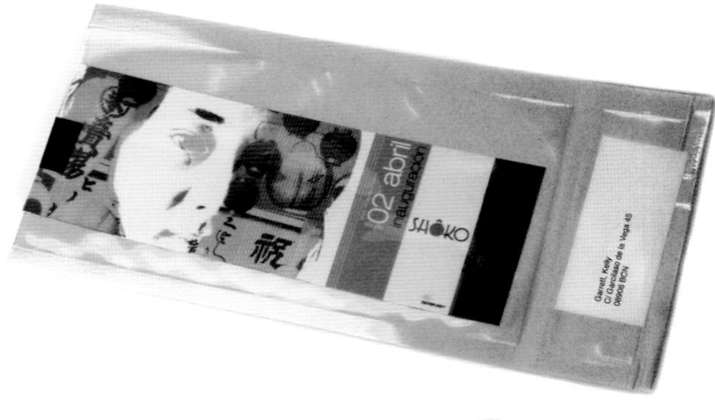

SigSagSug's
HEILIGER
BiMBAM
Samstag
4. Dezember 2004
ab 21.00 ★ 10.-
im Salzhaus Winterthur
dj Foxx &
dj Handssolo
vvk: SigSagSug oder starticket.ch
★ LEXX, SMASH FX & THE SHOWGIRLZ ★
SAMSTAG 20.3.2004
AB 23 UHR
ROUGH!
BREAKBEATS & DISCOTEK
WWW.MASCOTTE.CH mascotte BELLEVUE ★ ZURICH

Discothèque | Barcelona | Stuart Patterson

Discothèque | Barcelona | Toni Colomar

Gay Day @ Space | Barcelona | David Cantero

Cathedral Sundays | Barcelona | Neus Cardona
The Endup | San Francisco | theendup.com

Velvet
underground
Sidecar
FACTORY CLUB
TM
POKER CLUB
en FELLINI
KEN
Sky funk
MIAMI
EVERY SATURDAY - DOWNSTAIRS TERRA
La Paloma
UNIQUE
Beau Monde
la boîte
Bongo Lounge
333 Sat
The CATWALK
CLUB
SIROCO
Gay Day
SHÔKO
Fiesta de los Maniques
en FELLINI
NEON
COCOON BCN
en plan TRAVESTI
the Boiler
LOKOTRON
ZOUK
electri
aqualand
octopussy
club FELLINI
DISCOTHEQUE D
la terrrazza
atmospherical fun club
1 YEAR ON THE GROUND
Mond CLUB
THE ROOM
PACHA
BARCELONA
DIRTY DANCING
La Paloma
freak bar
Bateau River's King
BELLEVUE · ZÜRICH
CABARE

LOGOS +TYPOGRAPHY

Todo club tiene un nombre y un logotipo que le identifica y le distingue de los demás. El logotipo será el motivo a repetir en todos y cada uno de los flyer que el diseñador tenga que crear para el club para el que está trabajando. Cuando hablamos de logo no sólo vamos a fijarnos en el logotipo del club, sino en todos aquellos elementos que cada diseñador va a seleccionar, un objeto o imagen además del logo oficial, que serán repetidos durante toda la temporada, consiguiendo que el cliente rápidamente asocie la imagen que está viendo con el flyer de su club favorito.
Un montón de palabras y logotipos atrapados en un pequeño trozo de papel podría ir en contra de todas las reglas del diseño convencional, pero en el caso del diseño de flyers, ese problema carece de total importancia, y cobra en sí mismo todo el sentido del mundo.
En algunas ocasiones...
...¡Una palabra vale más que mil imágenes!

All clubs, without exception, have a name and a logo by which they are identified and distinguished from others. The logo is the motif found on each and every one of the flyers which the designer creates for the club for which he is working. When we speak of the logo, we are not only referring to the club's logo, but all the elements which each designer chooses whether they be objects or images to add to the official logo which will be repeated throughout the season, the client as a result will rapidly associate the image with his or her favourite club.
A plethora of words and logos captured on a small piece of paper could very easily go against all the rules of conventional design,
but in the case of flyer designs, this problem rather than being somewhat less relevant, takes on all the significance in the world.
At times...
...A single word is worth more than a thousand images!

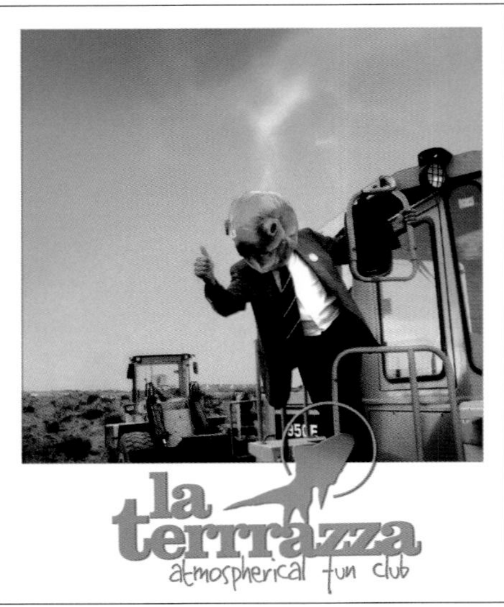

La Terrazza I Barcelona I Jaime Razquin

La Terrazza | Barcelona | Jaime Razquin

Bateau River's King | Paris | Cédric Melou

MAZI
MYNC PROJECT
JAMES HOLDEN
DERRICK CARTER
17
JIAK KIM STREET
SINGAPORE 169420
6738 2988
WWW.ZOUKCLUB.COM
ZOUK
IT'S FREE!
DJ/EVENT SCHEDULE FOR 20 - 28 JUNE
JAMES HOLDEN UK
SATURDAY 28 JUNE 2003 AT ZOUK
JAMES
HOLDEN
At just twenty-three years of age, James Holden has made an impact on the dance music scene which many an older producer and DJ can only dream of. He has already produced a string of outstanding tracks, including his latest single Nothing on loaded records, which has received rave reviews in all the major dance music magazines, and has been hammered by the likes of Tiesto, Pete Tong, Howells, Lawler, and Hernan Cattaneo. A wizard with the FX pedal, he has also turned out equally stunning remixes for New Order, collaborated with Sasha, secured DJ residencies across Europe, and toured across the world. Don't miss this opportunity to catch this rising star in our global dance scene!
THIRTY THREE
13
WE ♥ HOUSE WITH DJ B &
DERRICK CARTER US
FRIDAY 27 JUNE 2003 AT ZOUK
Hailing from the Chicago house scene, but having a strong presence in today's global arena, Derrick Carter's music is all about feeling good. Although his sets are rooted in house, Derrick Carter freely travels outside club tastes, seamlessly incorporating old-school disco, soul, jazz, funk, and whatever else catches his fancy. After a long 5 year wait for fans, Carter released 'Square Dancing In A Round House' - his debut album which featured everything from awe-inspiring, old school Chicago anthems to new-wave jack grooves, a sheer musical diversity that set a new benchmark in the history of house music. Together with his UK-based imprint Classic adding to his growing notoriety in production talent, he has definitely become a celebrity among dance-music aficionados all over the world.
HMV Essential listening:
Derrick Carter - Square Dancing In A Round House (Classic)
11
DERRICK
CARTER

Zouk Club | Singapore | Jimmy

Bateau River's King | Paris | Cédric Melou

extraID
WORLD SERIES
Winston Hazel
(Afro Art, Moloko Tour DJ, UK)
Tadeu Nice (Deep Inc., LT)
Noisy (LT)
01.30
Friday
extraID
WORLD SERIES
free entrance with extra ID
Club Gravity Jasinskio str. 16, LT-2001 Vilnius, Lithuania
Entrance prices: 15 Lt members 20 Lt with flyer 25 Lt others
Entrance from Gele , inis Vilkas street Tel +370 5 2497966 info@clubgravity.lt

Ax Botar
(Love Parade, Berlin)
Tadeu Nice
(Deep Inc., LT)
Friday
03.26
Club Gravity · Jasinskio str. 16, Vilnius, Lithuania
Entrance prices: 15 Lt members ·
20 Lt with flyer · 25 Lt others
Entrance from Geležinis Vilkas street ·
Tel +370 5 2497966 · info@clubgravity.lt
extraID
WORLD SERIES
free entrance with extra ID

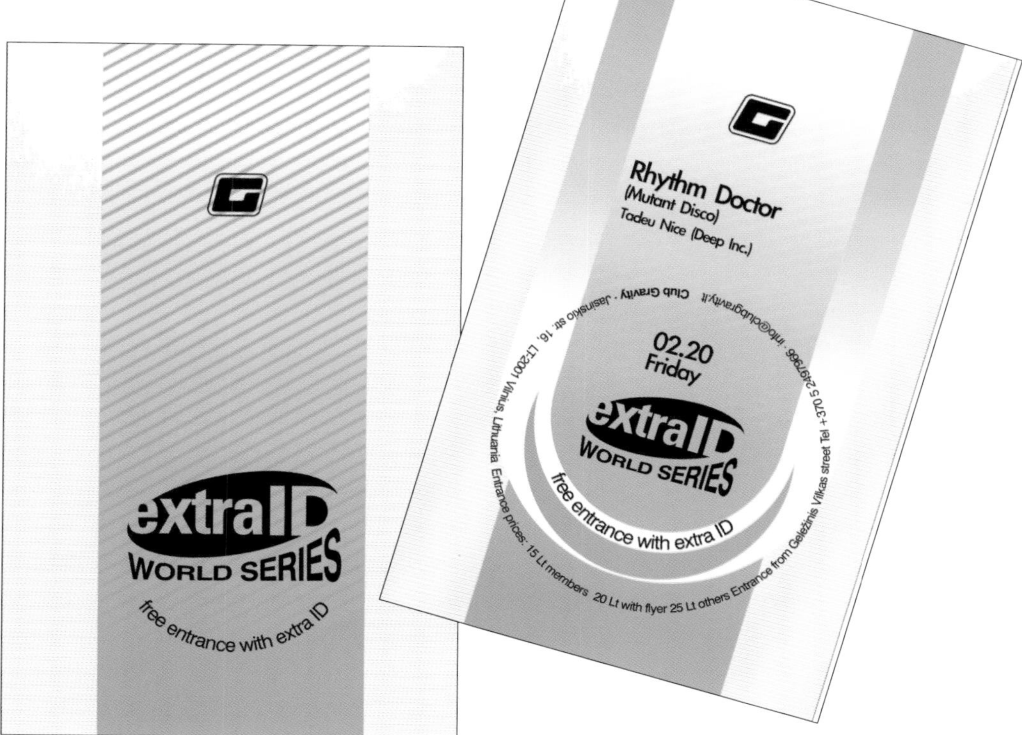

extraID
WORLD SERIES
free entrance with extra ID
Rhythm Doctor
(Mutant Disco)
Tadeu Nice (Deep Inc.)
02.20
Friday
extraID
WORLD SERIES
free entrance with extra ID

Club Gravity I Vilnius, Lithuania I clubgravity.lt

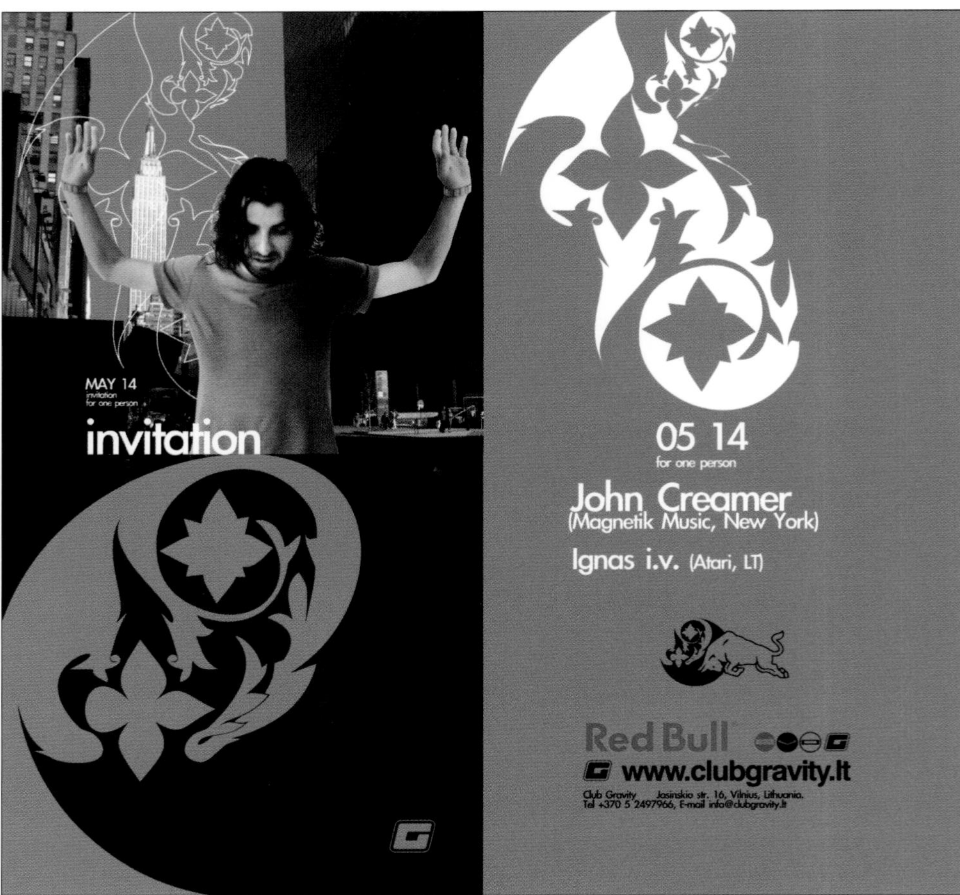

MAY 14
invitation
for one person
invitation
05 14
for one person
John Creamer
(Magnetik Music, New York)
Ignas i.v. (Atari, LT)
Red Bull
www.clubgravity.lt
Club Gravity Jasinskio str. 16, Vilnius, Lithuania.
Tel +370 5 2497966, E-mail info@clubgravity.lt

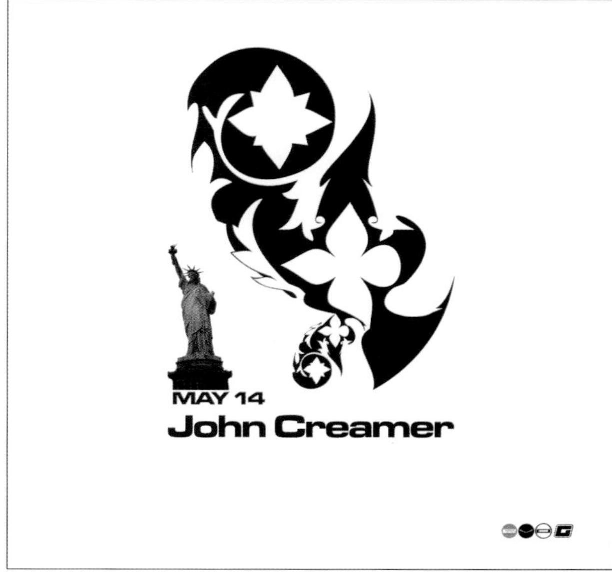

Club Gravity | Vilnius, Lithuania | clubgravity.lt

06 25 FRIDAY

PeeP!

Shooting Electro Stars

06 25 FRIDAY

PeeP!

Shooting Electro Stars

www.clubgravity.lt

Club Gravity · Jasinskio str. 16, Vilnius, Lithuania,
Tel +370 5 2497966, info@clubgravity.lt

la java.
wax présente les soirées
MATADOR
La Java 105 rue du fbg du temple
Paris 10 - Métro Belleville
TOUS LES VENDREDIS
DE DECEMBRE -21H-6H
8 EUROS

la java.
wax présente les soirées
MATADOR
La Java 105 rue du fbg du temple
Paris 10 - Métro Belleville
TOUS LES VENDREDIS
DE DECEMBRE 21H-6H
8 EUROS

la java.
wax présente les soirées
MATADOR
La Java 105 rue du fbg du temple
Paris 10 - Métro Belleville
TOUS LES VENDREDIS
DE DECEMBRE 21H-6H
8 EUROS

la java.
wax présente les soirées
MATADOR
La Java 105 rue du fbg du temple
Paris 10 - Métro Belleville
TOUS LES VENDREDIS
DE DECEMBRE 21H-6H
8 EUROS

La Java | Paris | Klem

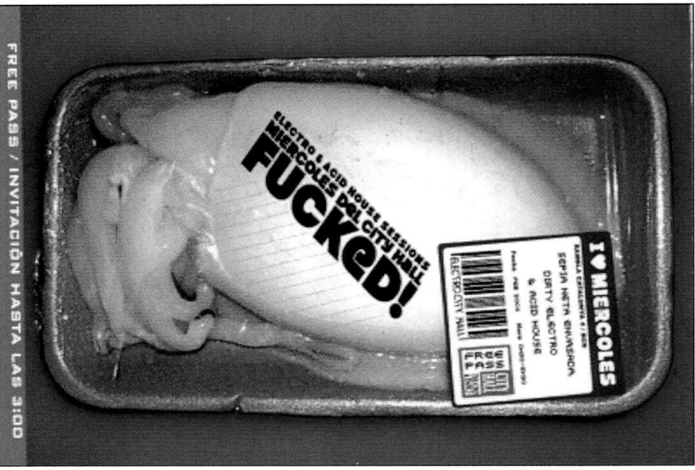

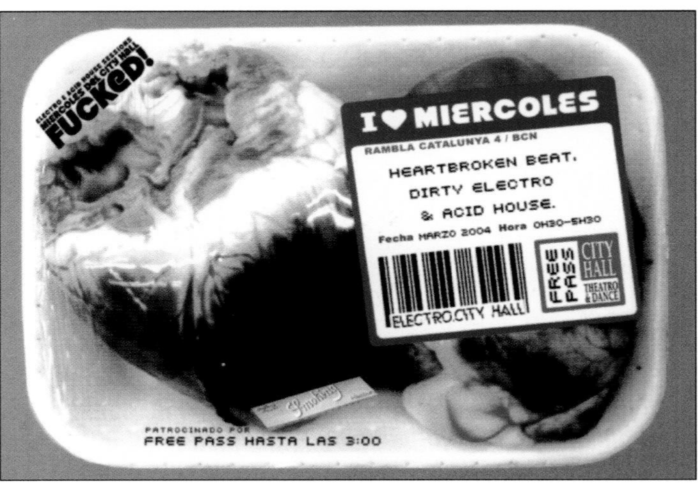

City Hall | Barcelona | Lauren Zac

Peach Club | Barcelona | Toni Colomar

Point Ephemere | Paris | Marie is not dead

electrochock★★★ présente

PIN'UPS LOVE FRENCH THUGS

LIVE:

GREMS aka SUPERMICRO & DATA+ guests
(Deep hop / Paris)

FUCK A LOOP
(Institubes / Paris)

Dj set by Diaz & Die2Die

SAMEDI 18 JUIN

21h / 2H
8 euros
Point Ephémère
200 quai de valmy
75010 Paris
métro : Jaurès

pointephemere.org
electrochock.com

POINT EPHÉMÈRE

DESIGN: MARIEISNOTDEAD@HOTMAIL.COM

LUMIERE NOIRE 4

Nouveau Casino

SAMEDI 31 JUILLET 2004

00H00 / 06H00 – 5 EUROS AVANT 01h, PUIS 10 EUROS

Noveau Casino | Paris | Cédric Melou

Danceclassics &
les meilleurs Slows
la Boum
présenté par Felix, Marcel, Pierre
et les "Taxidancers"

Neon
Electro!!!
Neon Thursdays at JaiBar
With tiga & justin

April 26
ビデオボーイ
8
electroFunkyBeatsAlaNewWave
マジで!
VBアイドル総勢15人が体験した
Hで身も凍る様な怪奇現象とは!
私、幽霊にイタズラ
With special guest dj
COVERgirl:
サヨナラヌード
麻生早苗
夕樹舞子
No.1スレンダーのピンナップ
今月のポスターカレンダー
小川明日香
小室友里
Neon
Thursdays
椎名舞
井上詩織
類似シリーズ無制限1本勝負

NEON
Samedi 26 octobre
MärtiniBrös [Berlin] live
Pläy
Turbo
i NEON
GURU
BOISSON ENERGIE

J'
NEON SAT.AUG.30th2003

En estas páginas / These pages
Jai Bar | Montreal, Canada | Justin Dallegret
Páginas siguientes / Next pages
Jai Bar | Montreal, Canada | Justin Dallegret

Sat.jan.26th
NEON
Miss Kittin
& the Hacker
Sat 305 St.Catherine ouest
20.00$

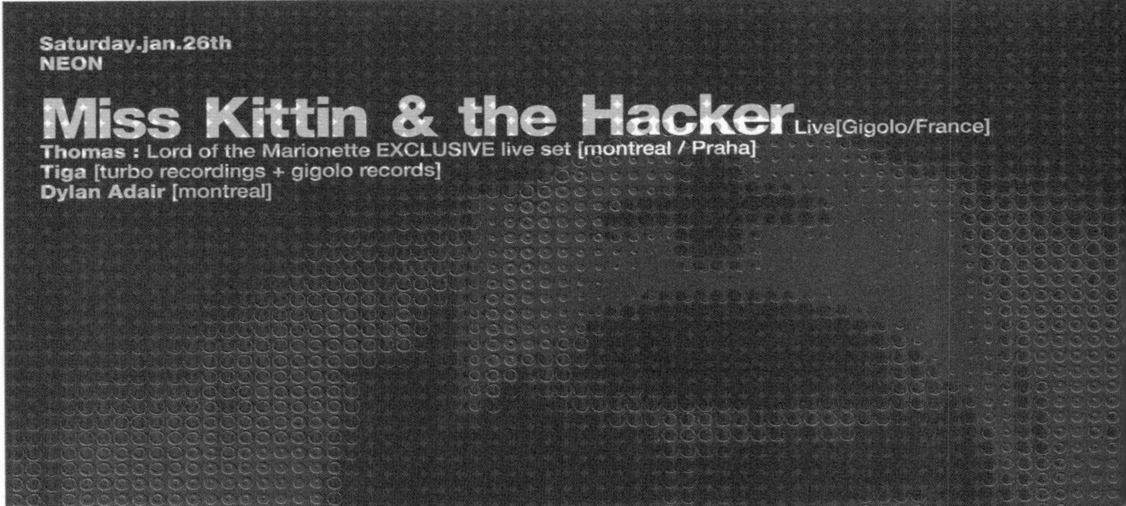
Saturday.jan.26th
NEON
Miss Kittin & the Hacker Live[Gigolo/France]
Thomas : Lord of the Marionette EXCLUSIVE live set [montreal / Praha]
Tiga [turbo recordings + gigolo records]
Dylan Adair [montreal]

Sat.jan.26th
NEON
Miss Kittin & the Hacker

i ♥
NEON

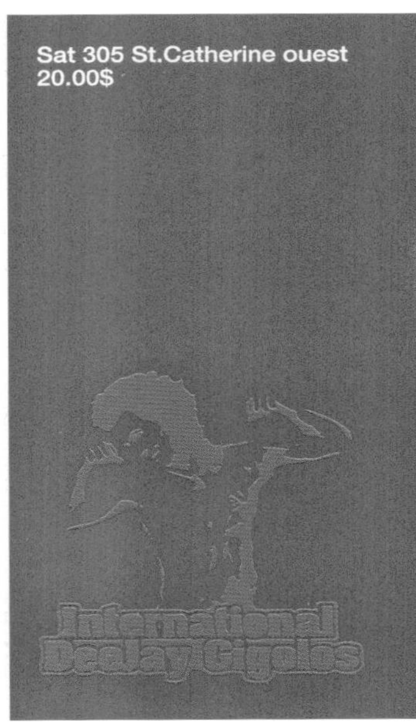
Sat 305 St.Catherine ouest
20.00$
International
Deejay Gigolos

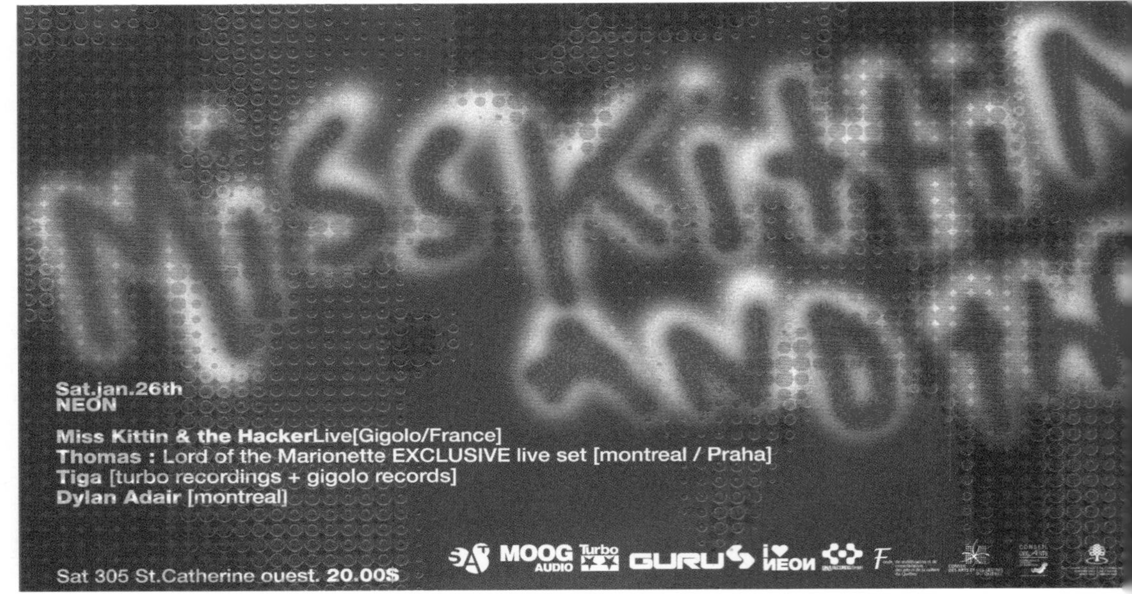
Sat.jan.26th
NEON
Miss Kittin & the HackerLive[Gigolo/France]
Thomas : Lord of the Marionette EXCLUSIVE live set [montreal / Praha]
Tiga [turbo recordings + gigolo records]
Dylan Adair [montreal]
Sat 305 St.Catherine ouest. 20.00$
MOOG AUDIO
Turbo
GURU
i ♥ NEON

Sat.jan.26th
NEON
Miss Kittin
& the Hacker

i ♥
NEON
Sat 305 St.Catherine ouest

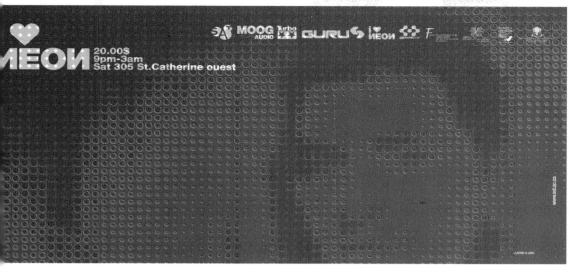

urday.jan.26th
ON

Miss Kittin & the Hacker Live[Gigolo/France]
omas : Lord of the Marionette EXCLUSIVE live set [montreal / Praha]
a [turbo recordings + gigolo records]
an Adair [montreal]

t 305 St.Catherine ouest 20.00$

www.sat.qc.ca

liss Kittin
the Hacker

Widenski
(Macadam Music, Estonia)
There are three DJ's having truly big disco music collection in Estonia. One of them is DJ Widenski.
Supacide (DK/LT)
04.03 Saturday
OLD DISCO
(UK) Marc Almond
Marc Almond, a vocalist from a legendary British duo SOFT CELL is very well known as a performer of 1981 hit 'Tainted Love' and cooperation with Jimmy Somerville 'I Feel Love'.
SOFT CELL established a style that was to influence several generations of musicians that followed - from PULP to BLUR, PET SHOP BOYS to THE DIVINE COMEDY.
Having published a book of poetry and biography, Mr. Almond is writing a book covering the most shocking and interesting sides of nightlife.
Is Gravity going to appear in the book?
What about you?
04.10 Saturday
TAINTED LOVE
P-Shaver (Partyzanai, LT)
SATURDAY NIGHT FEVER
All our March Saturdays are dedicated to disco and soulful house music.
Don't expect any progressive or techno house on that sweet March Saturday.
We will be pleased to provide you a cozy atmosphere, special dress code and superior aged drinks.
Strict face, dress and age control.
E-mail: saturday@clubgravity.lt
Club Gravity, Jasinskio str. 16, Vilnius
www.clubgravity.lt
SATURDAY NIGHT FEVER april
Ian Pooley
(Germany)
Over 50 remixes (featuring Bob Sinclair, X-PRESS2, DAFT PUNK, CARL COX, GREEN VELVET, THE CARDIGANS, MODJO...) and 3 albums has lead Ian Pooley from Detroito techno/house fan to deep disco house maestro and on the very top of international producers and DJ's.
There is going to appeer the fourth album by Ian Pooley in May (created in New Zealand and recorded in Sidney). On this LP expect more Brazilian and Latino influences... You'll be able to hear it three weeks before official album release... ;-)
ABSOLUT SECRETS
Entrance with invitations only.
04.17 Saturday
DANCING GLOBE #5
04.24 Saturday
Mystery Guest
SATURDAY NIGHT FEVER april
04.09 Friday
Jo Mills (UK)
Red Bull EVOLUTION
Ignas i.v. (Atari, LT)
Red Bull
Touch
(So Deep, Soulstice Entertainment, France)
Tadeu Nice (Deep Inc., LT)
TURNS ON THE MUSIC
CITY SPIRIT
Deep Soul Music All Night Long !
04.16 Friday
www.clubgravity.lt
Club Gravity · Jasinskio str. 16, Vilnius, Lithuania,
Entrance: 25 LTL, with flyer or EXTRA ID card (e.discount) 20 LT, members 15 LTL. First 50 clubbers only will enter the club for 10 LTL. Tel +370 5 2497966, info@clubgravity.lt
extra ID WORLD SERIES
Mr Willy (BOMFUNK MC'S, Finland)
04.23 Friday
04.30 Friday
ELECTRO NIGHT
APRIL FRIDAYS

Club Gravity | Vilnius, Lithuania | clubgravity.lt

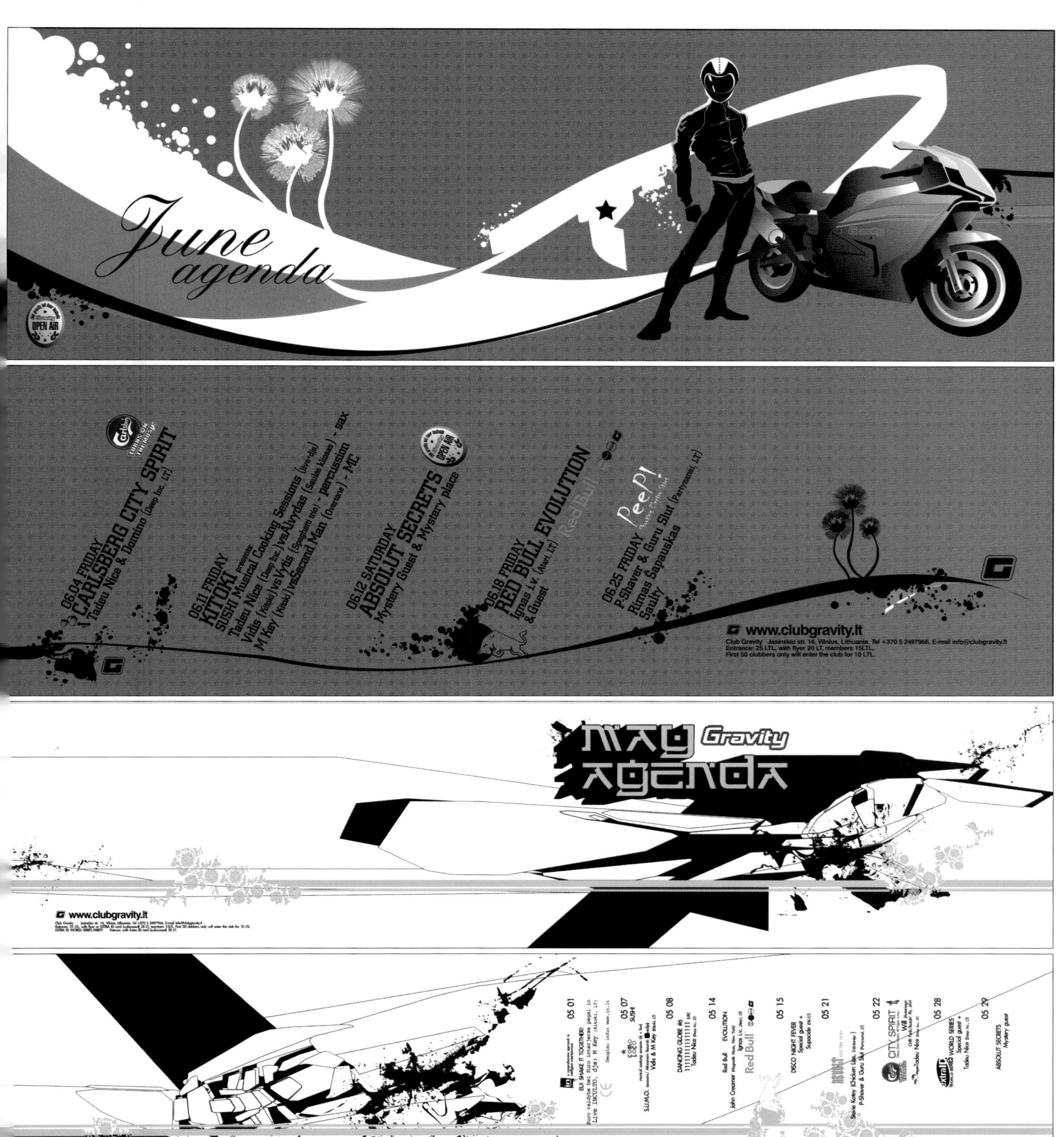

Club Gravity | Vilnius, Lithuania | clubgravity.lt

Rex Club | Paris | Grégoire Dalle
Club Mascotte | Zurich | Nadine Geissbühler
Página siguiente / Next page
Sweet Beat Records | Barcelona | Jordi Duró

ROCK'N'ROLL BLAST

THE ROOMATES

(UK) SWEET BEAT DOO WOPP RECORDING STARS

JETT DARREN & THE DOGGONE RIDERS

EL GRUPO DE ROCKABILLY MÁS ESPERADO
PRESENTANDO SU LP EN EL TORO RECORDS

DJ'S: FRANTIC AL + EDDIE
SÁBADO 17 FEBRERO
A PARTIR DE LAS 10
EN THE OTHER PLACE,
C/ PUJADES 226
(JUNTO METRO POBLE NOU)
ENTRADA: 2.000 PTA.

sweet BEAT records

THE OTHER PLACE BARCELONA

Club Fellini | Barcelona | Manel Moedano

Club Fellini | Barcelona | Manel Moedano

RAMONES
DAS
MUSICAL
GABBA
GABBA
HEY
starring
Rolf Zacher, Ades Zabel u.a.
Inszenierung
Jörg Buttgereit
musikalische Leitung
Tommy Ramone
arrangiert von
Nick Sheppard
(Ex- The Clash)
A LOWER EAST SIDE LOVE STORY
Samstag 15. &
Sonntag 16. Oktober
DOORS 19 30 SHOW 20 30
very special guests
Rams (Bucks) & Grau (Fleisch)
BELLEVUE · ZÜRICH
VVK: STARTICKET.CH, JAMARICO-ZH, BIZZ, JELMOLI- & MIGROS-CITY, MANOR, ROCKAWAY BEACH (BE), MATA HARI BAR (ZH), KLANGUNDKLEID.CH
EVENTIM-Hotline: 01805 - 570 000 (0,12 EUR / Min.) www.eventim.de & www.getgo.de
ROCKAWAY BEACH
KLANGUNDKLEID.CH
RockStar
Mata Hari
Langstr. 237, Zürich
CONVERSE

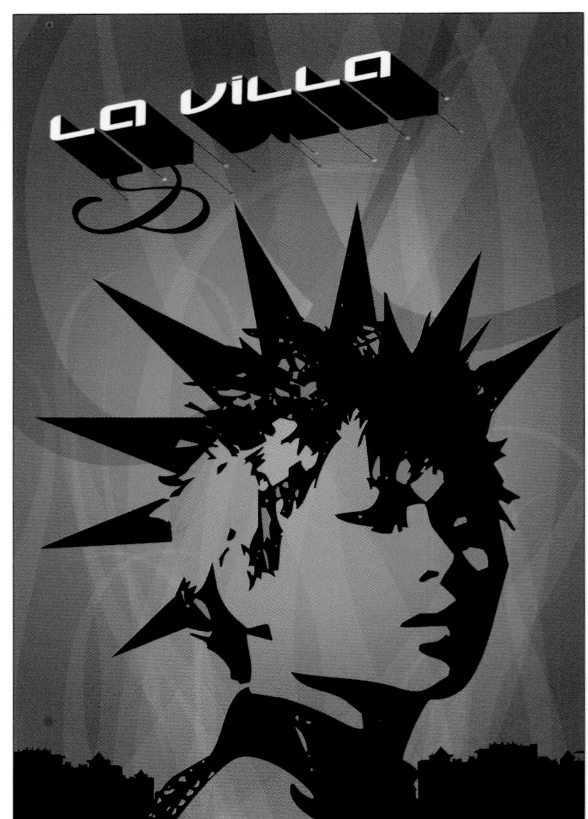
LA VILLA

VVK: WWW.STARTICKET.CH (0900 325 325), BIZZ, JELMOLI- & MIGROS-CITY, MANOR
SAMSTAG 22.1.2005 ★ DOORS 21 00 ★ CONCERT 22 00
PEACHES
TAYLOR SAVVY GONZALES
AS
FEEDOM
live!
KOOK & ROXXY (BERLIN) live!
FIEBERTANZ DJ.SET (D) & VASCOCK DJ. (ZH)
VISUALS BY
BLAUTON.ORG, THOMAS KAUFMANN & SOLEDADNODUELE.CH
BELLEVUE MASCOTTE ZURICH
Carlsberg Beer

LA VILLA

En esta página / This page
Beach Club | Zurich | Nadine Geissbühler
Crobar | New York City | crobar.com
Página izquierda / Left page
Club Mascotte | Zurich | Nadine Geissbühler
La Villa | Paris | Bastin Christophe

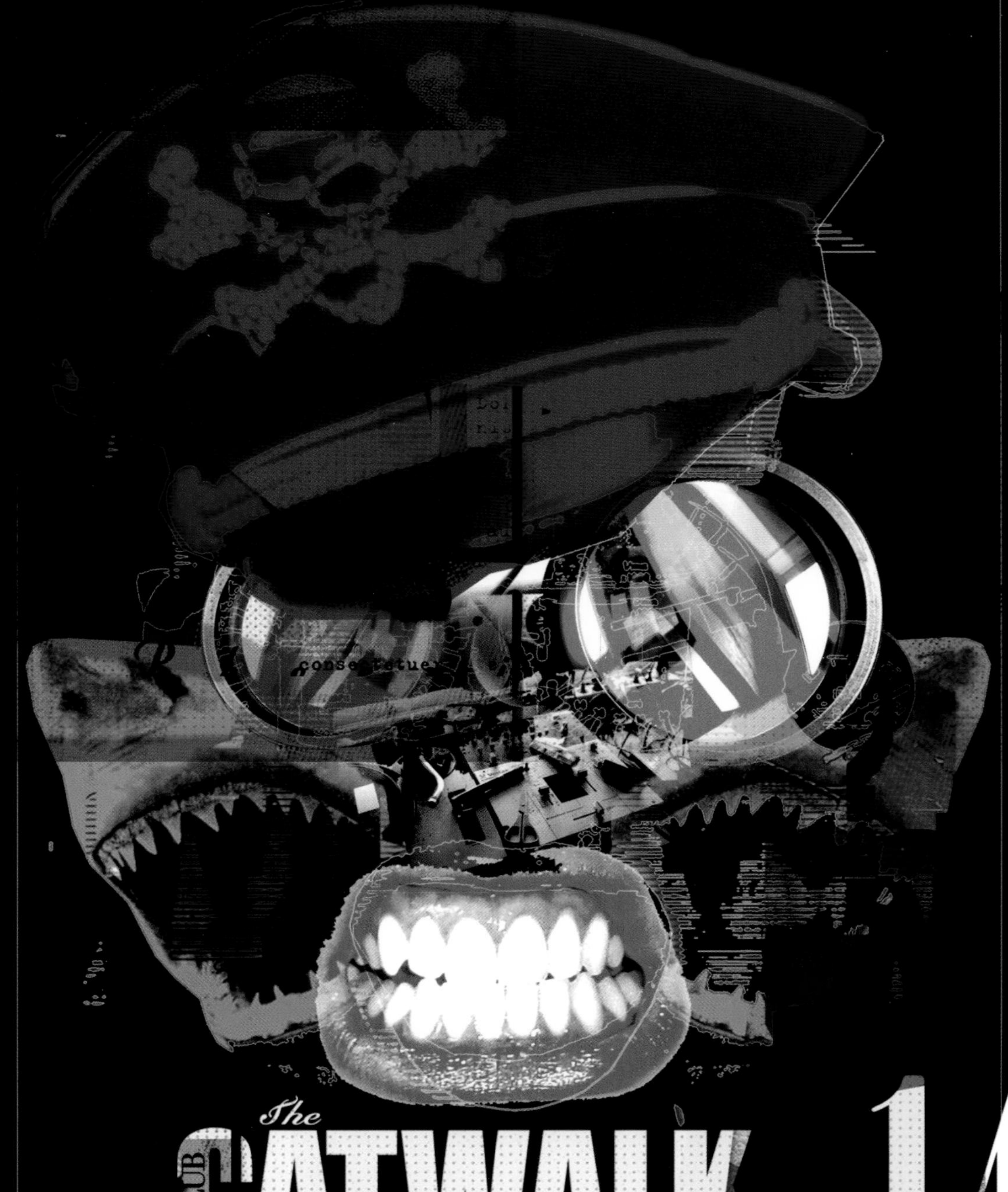
The
CLUB CATWALK
14
ENERO
primer
ANIVERSARIO
de club catwalk BCN

En estas páginas / These pages
Club Catwalk I Barcelona I Oscar Cardó

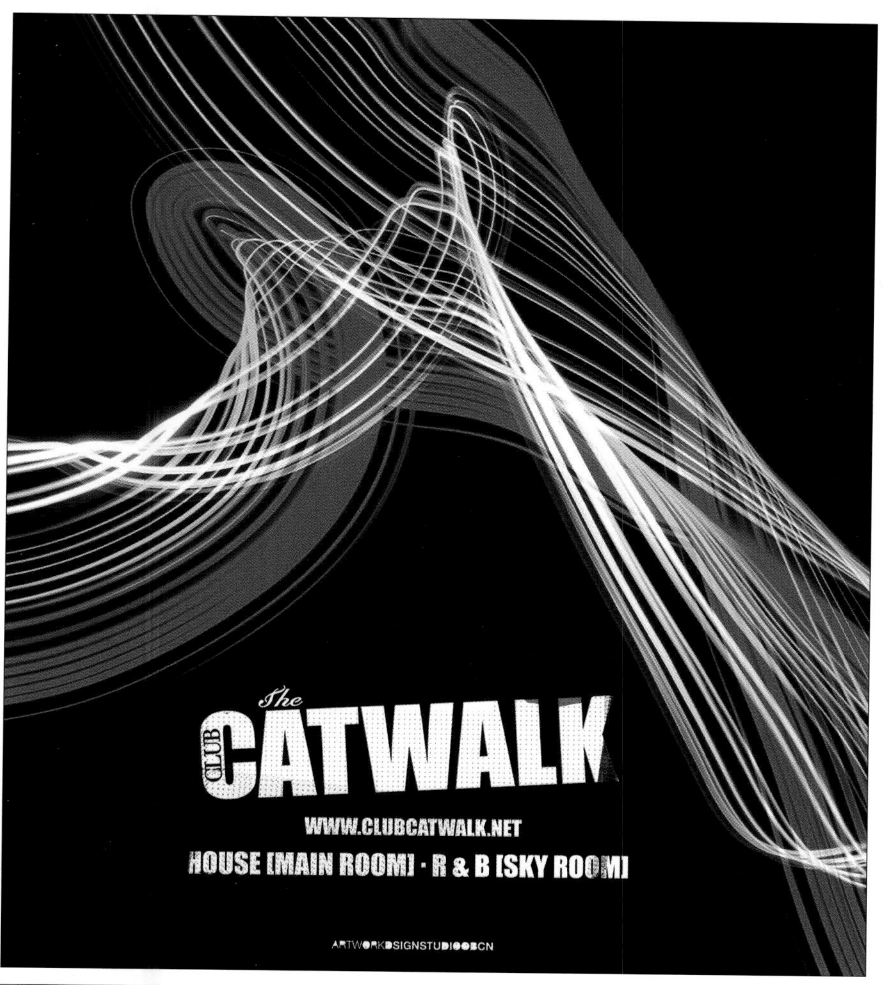

OPEN
7
DAYS!

THURSDAY JANUARY 20
DANCETERIA PRESENTS
THE FIRE SHOW

HAPPY
BIRTHDAY!
D
Danceteria
30 W 21st NYC 10010

All Stars Dj's Festival | Barcelona | Toni Colomar
Sugar La Baule | Paris | The Fly Designers

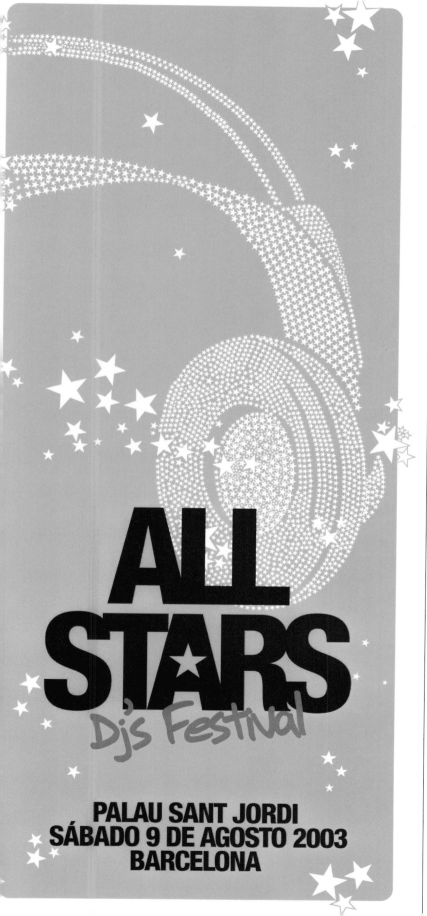

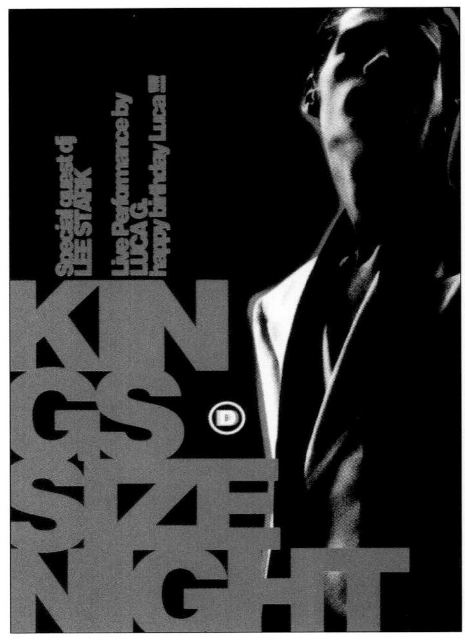

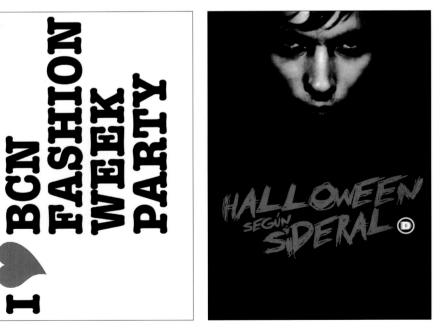

En estas páginas / These pages
Discothèque I Barcelona I Toni Colomar

CARNAVAL
SUPER
POP
FRAN
CESCO
FARFA
VIERNES
20 FEB
2004

THE
BEST
NEW
YEAR'S
EVE 2004

SMOKIN JO

YOU KEN DO it! best remixes

ken

WHO LOVES YOU?

Página izquierda / Left page
Ken Tour | Hollywood | Stuart Patterson
En esta página / This page
Loveball 2005 | Brussels | Stuart Patterson
Discothèque | Barcelona | Stuart Patterson
Penelope | Ibiza | Stuart Patterson

SUNDAY 7TH AUGUST
LOVEBALL PREVIEW PARTY!
KEN

ACAPULCO BAR · NEUGASSE 56 · 8005 ZÜRICH

En esta página / This page
Zac Club I Barcelona I Splik
Página izquierda / Left page
Acapulco I Zurich I Nadine Geissbühler

The

CLUB CATV

En estas páginas / These pages
Club Catwalk | Barcelona | Oscar Cardó

Catwalk | Barcelona | Oscar Cardó

Dada | Barcelona | Splik

ON NEWSSTANDS NOW!
COMING TO XBOX JUNE 7
Grand Theft Auto San Andreas
SAT JUNE 4
DOORS 11PM
SPIRIT
530 W 27
the junior vasquez EXPERIENCE
crobar
ADVANCE TICKETS AT CROBAR.COM
530 W 28TH ST NEW YORK CITY 212.629.9000
DEFMIX presents
Pre-Ibiza Indulgence!!!
Saturday, June 4
David Morales
Friday June 3rd
residency closing party
sandra collins
Fundacion
FRESH IN

La Paloma
SO REBEL! CLUB!
DIRTY ROTTEN DJ'S
SHINICHIRO SADAA DJ
RELEASE PARTY
KAOS feat. KHAN
SO REBEL! GUITARS
MAADRAASSOO + DJ NIÑO
CHEW THE FAT!
THE ROUGE ELEMENT
FETISCH
AN DER BEAT + SIDERAL
CARNAVAL LA PALOMA
SPORTING CLUB
CARNAVAL GAY
YOGA
1er Aniversario
Raval Launch
MIÉRCOLES 8 FEBRERO
KID LOCO
FEDERICO AUBELE
La Paloma

CLUB
picture
show
Molina
CLUB

liqui
Julio
Hugo delcano
SWAYZAK
Deepest
HD SUBSTANCE

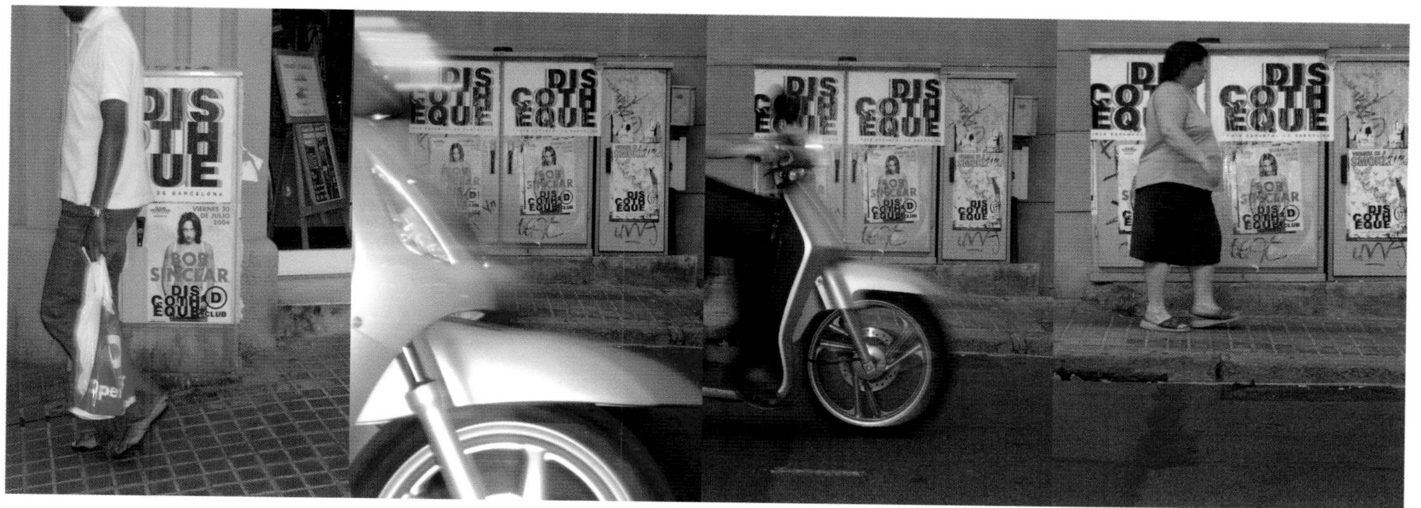

POSTERS

A menudo el flyer se convierte en póster, así que en principio se puede decir que un póster es un flyer de grandes dimensiones. Pero no es así, si el flyer pasa a ser póster pierde la esencia principal de su existencia, la de "volar". El impedimento del póster de ir de mano en mano, de tienda a bar, de bolsillo a la puerta del club, no es un factor que pueda determinar una falta de efectividad, sino todo lo contrario.

El póster asalta indiscriminadamente el paisaje urbano y le avalan siglos de experiencia. El transeúnte topa sin cesar con estos trozos de papel pegados a la superficie de los edificios de nuestras ciudades, su presencia en número es mayor que la del flyer y su ubicación más espontánea. En cualquier esquina, en puertas y escaparates de los comercios, en árboles, en cabinas telefónicas, buzones y contenedores de basura, en autobuses y en el metro, no podemos escapar a su presencia e influencia.

Su naturaleza está tan estrechamente vinculada a la vida moderna y de consumo que se creó un espacio único y privilegiado para su exhibición: la valla publicitaria.

La vida del póster ha corrido de la mano del devenir histórico y de los movimientos artísticos y así sigue comportándose. El flyer ha aprendido la lección rápido y en la actualidad se convierte en heredero directo del póster y en un testigo histórico y artístico excepcional.

The flyer often becomes a poster, which in principal it could be said a poster is just a large flyer. This is not the case, the flyer transformed into poster loses the main essence of its existence, that of being able to "fly". Whilst the posters inability to be passed from hand to hand, from shop to bar, from pocket to club door might appear to reduce its effectiveness, this is in fact quite the contrary.

Posters indiscriminately attack the urban environment endorsed as they are by endless experience.

A never ending barrage of these pieces of paper are to be seen plastered all over the buildings in our cities, their presence being greater in number than that of the flyers and their location more random. On every corner, on shop doors and windows, on trees, telephone cabins, mail boxes and rubbish containers, on the buses and in the metro, we are unable to escape neither their presence nor their influence.

Their nature is so closely linked to modern life and our consumer society that a unique and privileged space has been created for their exhibition: the billboard.

The poster's life has progressed at the hands of historical transformation and artistic movements and continues to do so. The flyer, having rapidly learnt the same lesson, has become a direct heir to the poster and an extraordinary historic and artistic witness.

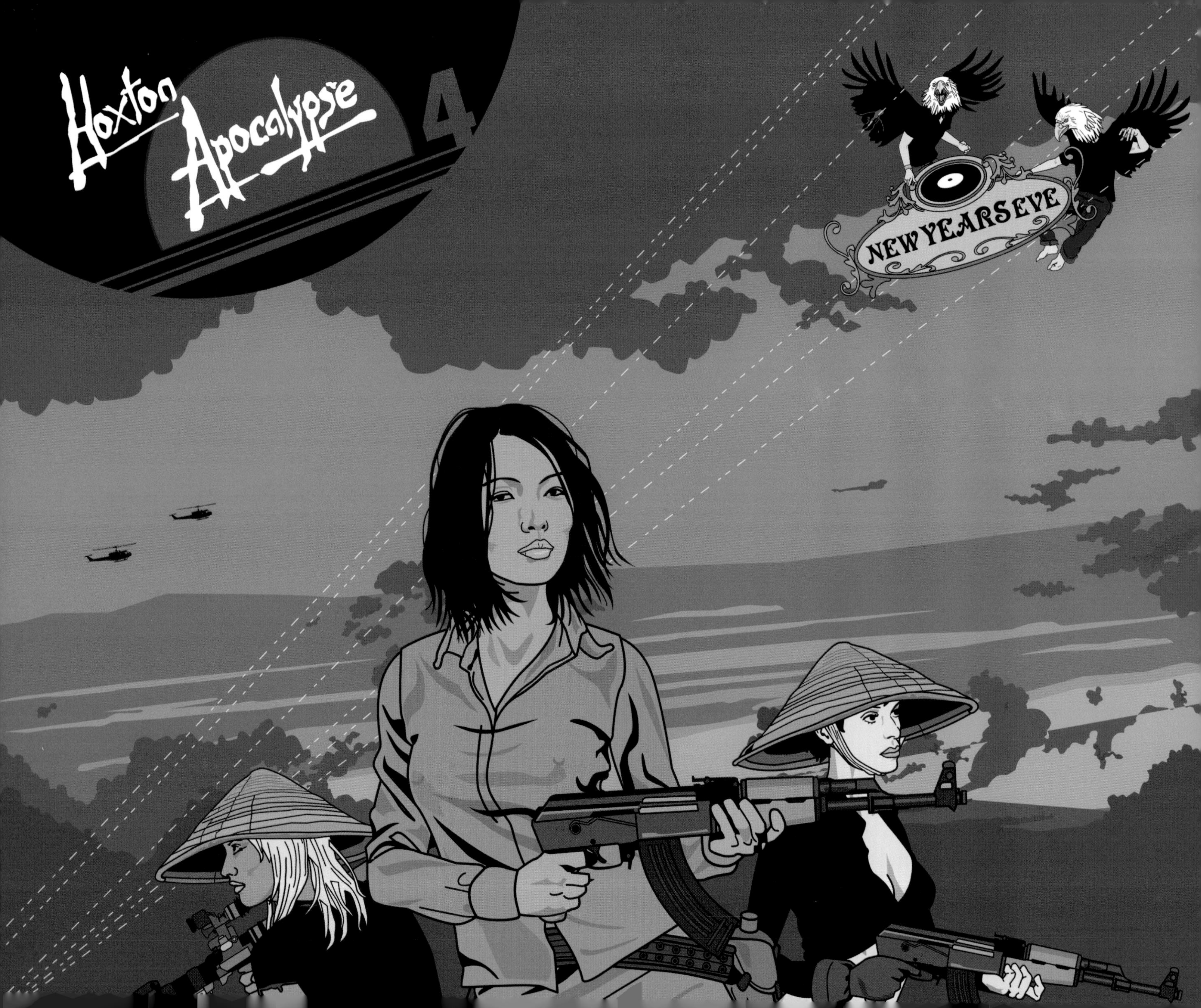
Hoxton Apocalypse
4
NEW YEARS EVE

En esta página / This page
333 Saturday's I London I Elliot Thoburn
Página siguiente / Next page
Club 13 I Barcelona I Silvia Prada

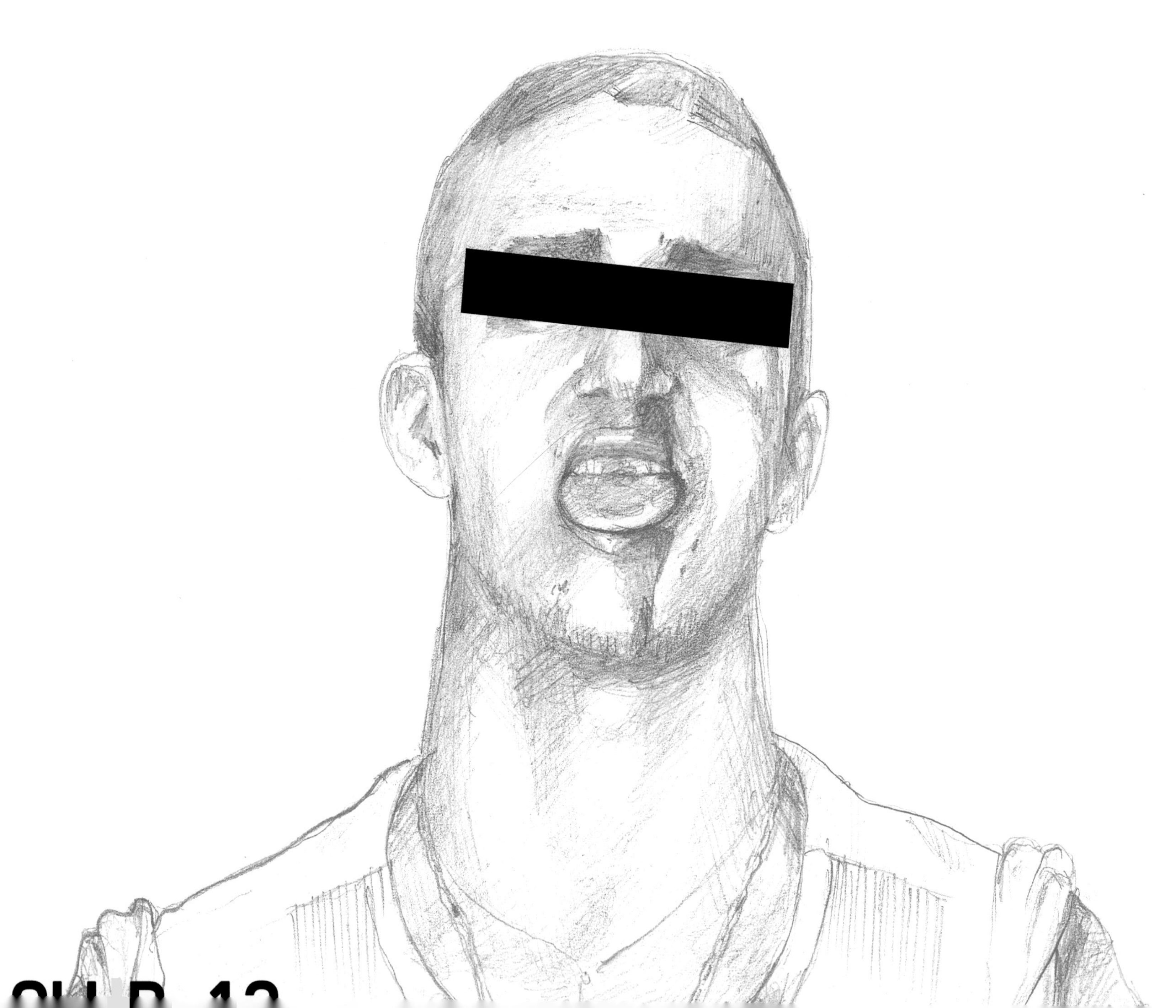

PLAZA REAL, 13
RESTAURANTE-TERRAZA-CLUB
MONDAY-TUESDAY-WEDNESDAY-THURSDAY-FRIDAY-SATURDAY-SUNDAY
TEL. 93 317 23 52
AHGGG
COLABORAN
Estrella Damm
Pepe Jeans LONDON
auping
GO PLAY Ballantine's
NØRDIC MIST

D: Jordi Duró P: Lee Friedlander (Ben E. King & LaVern Baker)

the Boiler

Rhythm and Soul Club
Saturday March 12th
from 24:00 until 5:00
5 euros

Guest DJs:
Damien Lapeyre
Bubblegum Weekend
La Rochelle
Bernat
Soul Affection
Lleida
Resident DJs:
Cristina Alonso
Jordi Duró

Sala Frank Dubé
Carrer Buscarons 18
Barcelona

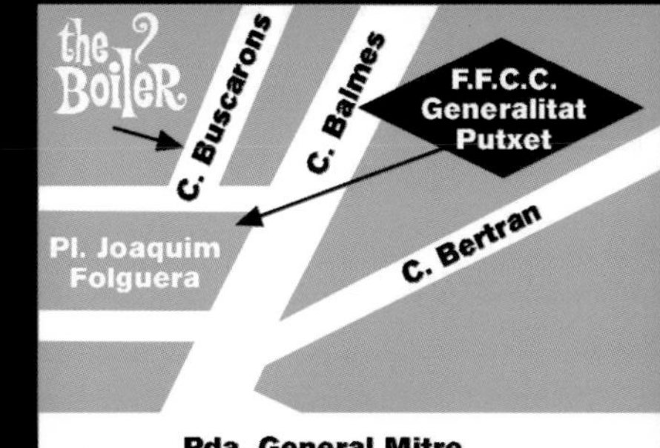

The Boiler | Barcelona | Jordi Duró
Páginas / Pages 106-107
Sidecar Factory Club | Barcelona | Jordi Duró
Páginas / Pages 108-109
Wigstock Festival | New York City | Scott Lifshutz

Penniman Records presenta

desde NY

THE A-BONES

+ Born Losers

Jueves 28 de Julio a las 22h

en Sidecar Factory Club (Plaza Real/BCN)

+ DJ Jordi Duró

Precio único: 12 euros

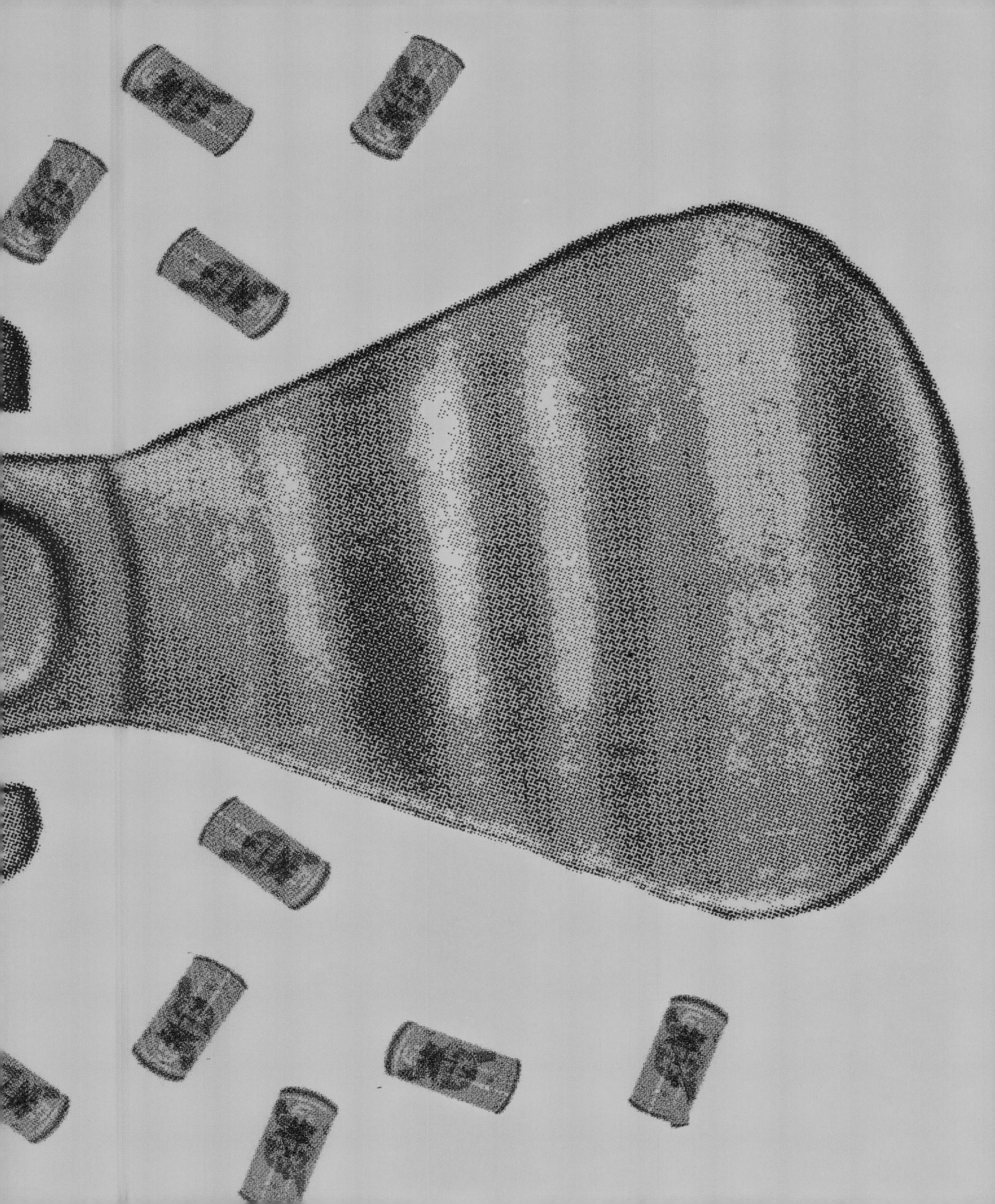

WiGSTOCK

2001

©ewalt

POWER GROOVE
La Paloma
SEPTIEMBRE 2004
VIERNES 3 01:30h
BARRIO!
KOSMOS + SIXISMOTIONGRAPHICS
(BREAKS & BEATS / BCN)
SÁBADO 4 02:00h
LA MALA FAMA
DJ'S PACO CLANDESTINO & CRISTIANO SPILLATI
(ECLÉCTICO / BCN)
VIERNES 10
MACARENA
DJ'S GABI & CARACOL
(FREESTYLE / BCN)
SÁBADO 11 02:00h
CLUB FRESH
DJ'S DANNY BRASCO + TONY 000
(HIP-HOP / BCN)
VIERNES 17
ASTON HARVEY FREESTYLERS
Featuring MC Sir REAL
(BIG BEAT / UK)
SÁBADO 18

Institut de cultura:
La Mercè
MIÉRCOLES 22 21:00h
GOVINDA (LIVE)
SIDONIE DJS + DJ GANESH & DJ MOS-KO
(ELECTRO - ASIAN FLAVOURS)
JUEVES 23 00:00h
BONGO LOUNGE
DILEMA "Black Style" + KUNTAKA "Raíces"
(FRESH SPANISH HIP HOP)
VIERNES 24 02:00h
+SPIRITUALIA+
ANDY DÁBULA + GROOVELAB BARCELONA + ETNOTRONIC
(ETNOTRONICA)
SÁBADO 25
RUDE DJ + NEW BLED VIBRATIONS
DJ AWAL & MC HICHAM
(NU EUROPE BEATS)
C/TIGRE 27 WWW.LAPALOMA-BCN.COM
OFICINA 933 177 994 SALA 933 016 897
SQUITX.NET

La Paloma | Barcelona | Squitx

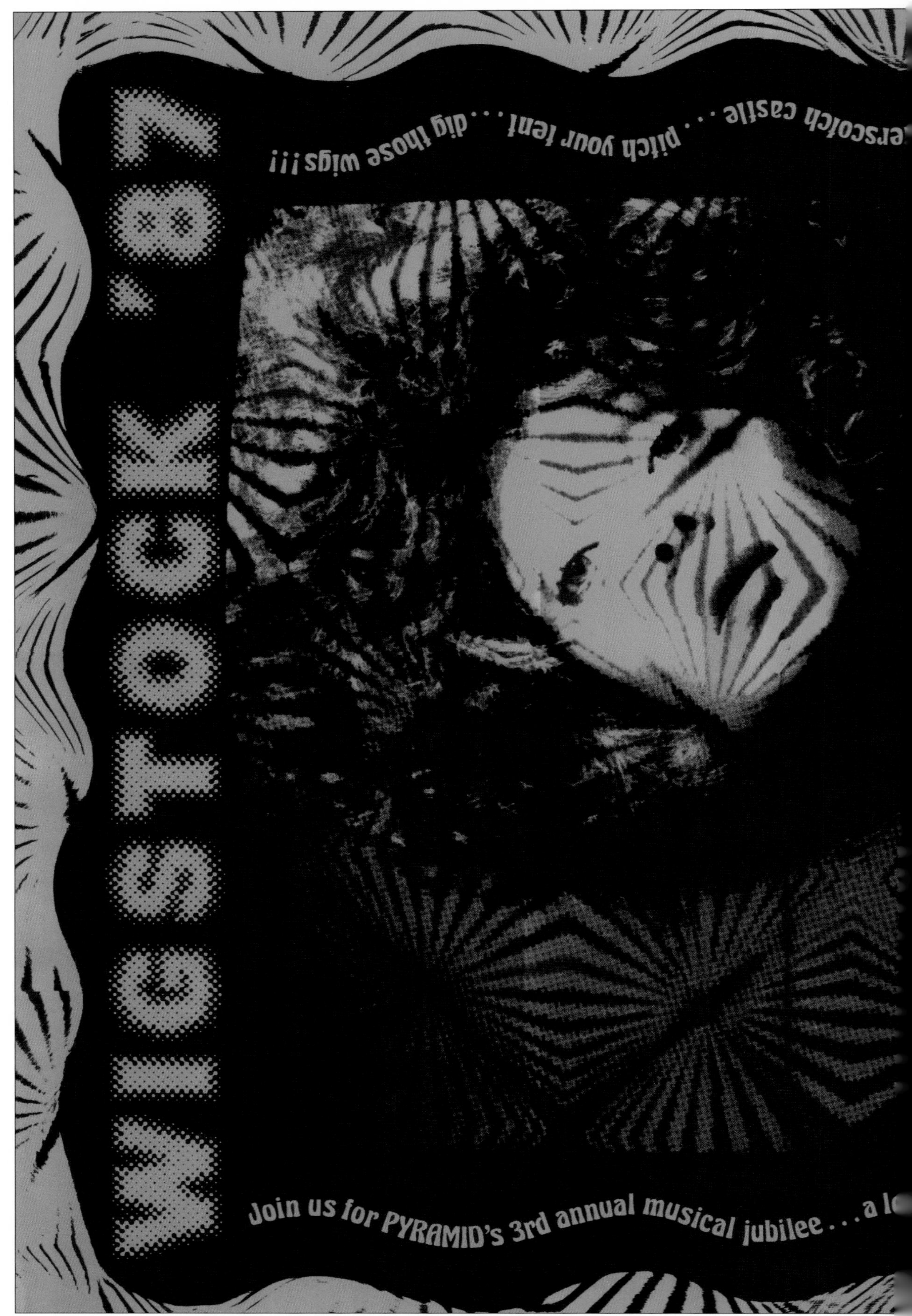
WIGSTOCK
Join us for PYRAMID's 3rd annual musical jubilee . . . a l
erscotch castle . . . pitch your tent . . . dig those wigs!!!

Wigstock Festival | New York City | Scott Lifshutz
Páginas / Pages 114-119
I Love Neon | USA | Justin Dallegret

I Love Neon

0 pm to 10 am, Bar & After
ontréal Canada - 32 Ste. Catherine West
nfo: www.iloveneon.ca

Main Room: 10pm -3am
DJ HELL (Germany)
TIGA (Turbo Recordings, Montreal)
JORDAN DARE
CUT THROAT
REPUBLIC LIVE
isuals: LE COUPLE

rigid Room: 10pm -3am
DJ FRIGID (www.djfrigid.com)
DJ CHERRY COLA

fter Hours: 3am - 10 am
TIGA
SEAN KOSA
MIGHTY KAT
VINCENT
LEMIEUX

0 pm to 10 am, Bar & After
ontréal Canada - 32 Ste. Catherine West
nfo: www.iloveneon.ca

Main Room: 10pm -3am
DJ HELL (Germany)
TIGA (Turbo Recordings, Montreal)
JORDAN DARE
CUT THROAT
REPUBLIC LIVE
isuals: LE COUPLE

rigid Room: 10pm -3am
DJ FRIGID (www.djfrigid.com)
DJ CHERRY COLA

fter Hours: 3am - 10 am
TIGA
SEAN KOSA
MIGHTY KAT
VINCENT
LEMIEUX

0 pm to 10 am, Bar & After
ontréal Canada - 32 Ste. Catherine West
nfo: www.iloveneon.ca

Main Room: 10pm -3am
DJ HELL (Germany)
TIGA (Turbo Recordings, Montreal)
JORDAN DARE
CUT THROAT
REPUBLIC LIVE
isuals: LE COUPLE

rigid Room: 10pm -3am
DJ FRIGID (www.djfrigid.com)
DJ CHERRY COLA

fter Hours: 3am - 10 am
TIGA
SEAN KOSA
MIGHTY KAT
VINCENT
LEMIEUX

I Love Neon

TIGA &
DJ HELL

VENDREDI LE 18 FEVRIER 2005
I LOVE NEON 10 PM TO 10 AM, BAR & AFTER
Montréal Canada - 32 Ste. Catherine West - info: www.iloveneon.ca

Main Room: 10pm- 3am
DJ HELL (International DJ Gigolos, Germany) **TIGA** (Turbo Recordings, Montreal) **JORDAN DARE** (White Leather Recordings, Montreal)
CUT THROAT REPUBLIC LIVE (Featuring Jordan Dare & Sean Kosa) **LE COUPLE** Visuals

Frigid Room:10pm- 3am
DJ FRIGID (www.djfrigid.com) **DJ CHERRY COLA**

After Hours: 3am - 10am
TIGA (Turbo Recordings, Montreal) 2nd set **SEAN KOSA** (White Leather Recordings, Montreal) **MIGHTY KAT** (dizzy, www.mightykat.com)
VINCENT LEMIEUX (Musique Risquée)

Montréal Canada - 32 Ste. Catherine West - info: www.iloveneon.ca

DJ HELL

(International DJ Gigolos, Germany)

Main Room:

TIGA (Turbo Recordings, Montreal) **JORDAN DARE** (White Leather Recordings, Montreal)

CUT THROAT REPUBLIC LIVE (Featuring Jordan Dare & Sean Kosa)

Visuals: **LE COUPLE**

Frigid Room: **DJ FRIGID** (www.djfrigid.com) **DJ CHERRY COLA**

After Hours:

TIGA (Turbo Recordings, Montreal) 2nd set

SEAN KOSA (White Leather Recordings, Montreal)

MIGHTY KAT (dizzy, www.mightykat.com)

VINCENT LEMIEUX (Musique Risquée)

Bar Tickets: 10 pm to 3 am
$15 + tx - advance pre-sale - At Moog/DNA Only - Available Thursday Jan 27th
$20 + tx - pre-sale / $25 + tx - at the door

After Hours Tickets: 3 am to 10 am (At the door only....)
$10 - with Neon ticket / $15 - without Neon ticket

Locations de prévente :
Admission : www.admission.com - 790-1245
Moog Audio/DNA Records: 3828 St-Laurent - 284-7434, Aritmetik Les Cours - 455 Rue Peel - 286-0565
Aritmetik St Denis - 2011 rue St-Denis - 847-8965 , Aritmetik St Laurent - 3688A St Laurent - 985-4130

www.iloveneon.ca
www.djhell.de
www.gigolo-records.de

DJ Hell is an innovator in the truest sense, having begun his mixing career while still a teenager. Hell has moved through punk and new wave to electro and hasn't stopped since. He has been DJ ing around the world for ever it seems and has produced some of Techno's most memorable tracks & owns one of the most important & influential record labels ever, International Deejay Gigolos. Gigolo is more or less the birthplace of modern electro, and has launched the careers of many artists such as Fisherspooner, Miss Kittin & The Hacker, Tiga, David Caretta, Vitalic, Zombie Nation & Crossover, to name a few.... Hell returns to Montreal & to NEON for the first time since 1999, this is going to be big.

réal Canada - 32 Ste. Catherine West - info: www.iloveneon.ca

Room:
J HELL (International DJ Gigolos, Germany) TIGA (Turbo Recordings, Montreal) JORDAN DARE (White Leather Recordings, Montreal)
UT THROAT REPUBLIC LIVE (Featuring Jordan Dare & Sean Kosa) Visuals: LE COUPLE
d Room:
J FRIGID (www.djfrigid.com) DJ CHERRY COLA
Hours:
GA (Turbo Recordings, Montreal) 2nd set SEAN KOSA (White Leather Recordings, Montreal) MIGHTY KAT (dizzy, www.mightykat.com)
NCENT LEMIEUX (Musique Risquée)

Tickets: 10 pm to 3 am
tx - advance pre-sale - At Moog/DNA Only - Available Thursday Jan 27th
tx - pre-sale
tx - at the door

Hours Tickets: 3 am to 10 am (At the door only....)
with Neon ticket
without Neon ticket

tions de prévente :
ssion : www.admission.com - 790-1245
g Audio/DNA Records: 3828 St-Laurent - 284-7434
etik Les Cours - 455 Rue Peel - 286-0565
etik St Denis - 2011 rue St-Denis - 847-8965
etik St Laurent - 3688A St Laurent - 985-4130

DJ HELL

FRIGID Recently acclaimed "DJ of the year" by ICI magazine, the androgynous Frigid cultivates ambiguity with a disarmingly outrageous approach. By giving new life to dance music, the electronic e... and performance art, Frigid brings a unique dimension to his work, inherited by the extravagance of the glam rock era.

Frigid returns to Neon for the first time since 2004's New Years Eve event to play alongside Tiga & DJ Hell in his very own frigid room with guest DJ Cherry Cola.

www.iloveneon.ca
www.djhell.de
www.gigolo-records.de

Bar Tickets: 10 pm to 3 am
$15 + tx - advance pre-sale - At Moog/DNA Only - Available Thursday Jan 27th
$20 + tx - pre-sale
$25 + tx - at the door

After Hours Tickets: 3 am to 10 am (At the door only....)
$10 - with Neon ticket
$15 - without Neon ticket

Locations de prévente :
Admission : www.admission.com - 790-1245
Moog Audio/DNA Records: 3828 St-Laurent - 284-7434
Aritmetik Les Cours - 455 Rue Peel - 286-0565
Aritmetik St Denis - 2011 rue St-Denis - 847-8965
Aritmetik St Laurent - 3688A St Laurent - 985-4130

SUN.MAR.27TH
I LOVE NEON
PRESENTS
NEON LOVE
+HEADMAN
+TIEFSCHWARZ
+SEAN KOSA
NEON LOVE
Locations de prévente :
17.50$+tx pré-vente - 21.75$+tx à la porte
S.A.T. 1195 St.Laurent - 844-2033 - www.sat.qc.ca
Moog Audio/DNA Records 3828 St-Laurent - 284-7434
Aritmetik Les Cours 455 Rue Peel - 286-0565
Aritmetik St Denis 2011 rue St-Denis - 847-8965
Lily Farouche 1042 mount-royal - 597-0202
I NEON
DIM.27 MARS
I LOVE NEON
PRESENTE
NEON LOVE
+HEADMAN
+TIEFSCHWARZ
+SEAN KOSA
visuels par "edonist"
Locations de prévente :
17.50$+tx pré-vente - 21.75$+tx à la porte
S.A.T. 1195 St.Laurent - 844-2033 - www.sat.qc.ca
Moog Audio/DNA Records 3828 St-Laurent - 284-7434
Aritmetik Les Cours 455 Rue Peel - 286-0565
Aritmetik St Denis 2011 rue St-Denis - 847-8965
Lily Farouche 1042 mount-royal - 597-0202
SAT
1195 St.Laurent
22h - 03h
www.iloveneon.ca

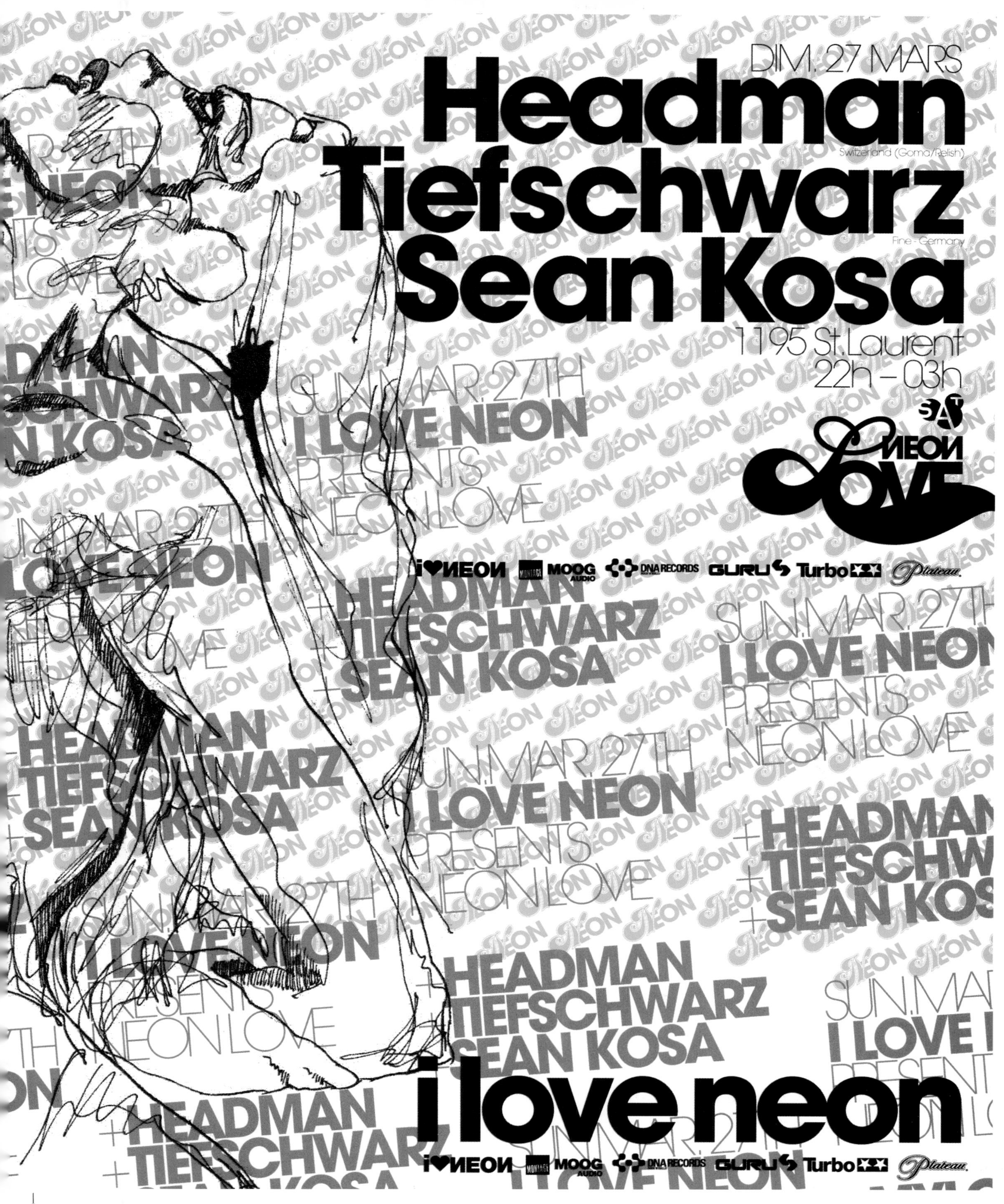
DIM. 27 MARS
Headman
Switzerland (Gomma/Relish)
Tiefschwarz
Fine - Germany
Sean Kosa
1195 St.Laurent
22h – 03h
SAT
NEON LOVE
SUN.MAR.27TH
I LOVE NEON
PRESENTS
NEON LOVE
HEADMAN
TIEFSCHWARZ
SEAN KOSA
i love neon
MOOG AUDIO
DNA RECORDS
GURU
Turbo
Plateau

Sat.Nov. 24th
American Gigolo: The Launch Party
SAT 305 St. Catherine west
9pm-3am/15$
i ♥ NEON

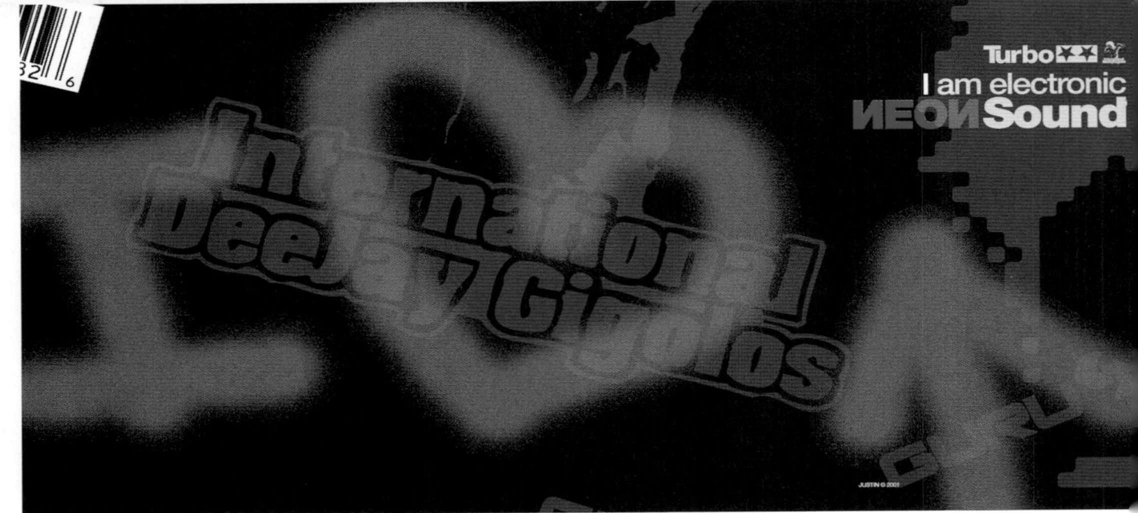
Turbo
I am electronic
NEON Sound
International Deejay Gigolos
JUSTIN © 2001

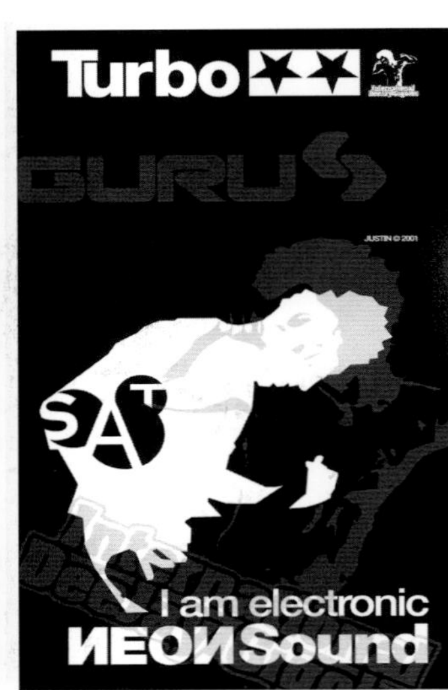
Turbo
GURUS
JUSTIN © 2001
SAT
I am electronic
NEON Sound

GURUS
NEON
JUSTIN © 2001 i ♥ NEON

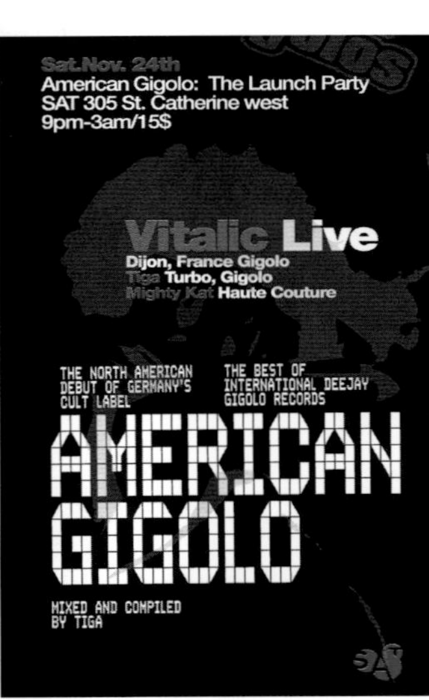
Sat.Nov. 24th
American Gigolo: The Launch Party
SAT 305 St. Catherine west
9pm-3am/15$
Vitalic Live
Dijon, France Gigolo
Tiga Turbo, Gigolo
Mighty Kat Haute Couture
THE NORTH AMERICAN DEBUT OF GERMANY'S CULT LABEL
THE BEST OF INTERNATIONAL DEEJAY GIGOLO RECORDS
AMERICAN GIGOLO
MIXED AND COMPILED BY TIGA

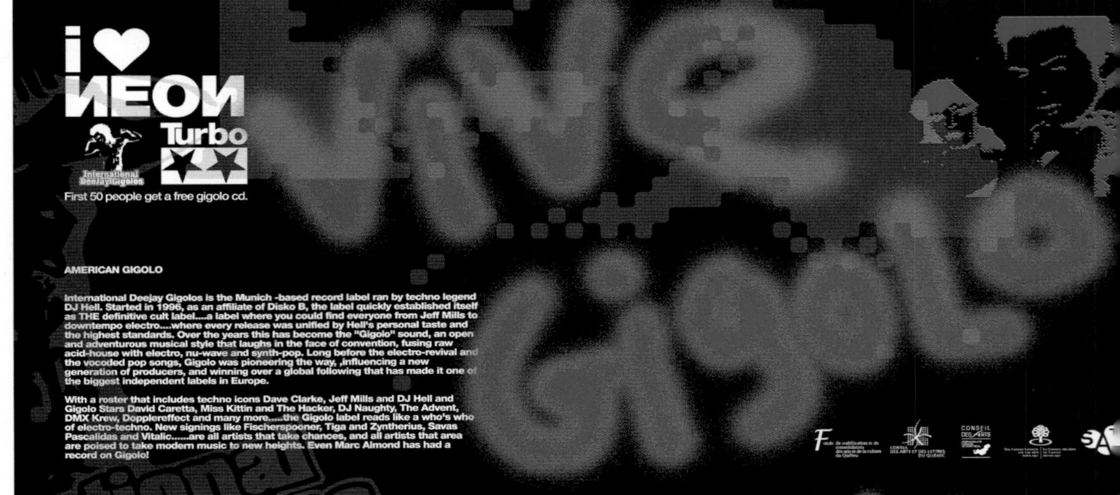
i ♥ NEON
Turbo
International Deejay Gigolos
First 50 people get a free gigolo cd.
AMERICAN GIGOLO
International Deejay Gigolos is the Munich -based record label ran by techno legend DJ Hell. Started in 1996, as an affiliate of Disko B, the label quickly established itself as THE definitive cult label....a label where you could find everyone from Jeff Mills to downtempo electro.....where every release was unified by Hell's personal taste and the highest standards. Over the years this has become the "Gigolo" sound, an open and adventurous musical style that laughs in the face of convention, fusing raw acid-house with electro, nu-wave and synth-pop. Long before the electro-revival and the vocoded pop songs, Gigolo was pioneering the way, ,influencing a new generation of producers, and winning over a global following that has made it one of the biggest independent labels in Europe.
With a roster that includes techno icons Dave Clarke, Jeff Mills and DJ Hell and Gigolo Stars David Caretta, Miss Kittin and The Hacker, DJ Naughty, The Advent, DMX Krew, Dopplereffect and many more.....the Gigolo label reads like a who's who of electro-techno. New signings like Fischerspooner, Tiga and Zyntherius, Savas Pascalidas and Vitalic......are all artists that take chances, and all artists that area are poised to take modern music to new heights. Even Marc Almond has had a record on Gigolo!

to stay in touch with our events, or if you just want to help out and be apart of us, email us
ilovemyneon@mac.com
i ♥ NEON

i feel electronik
ilovemyneon@mac.com
fastForward
ilovemyneon@mac.com

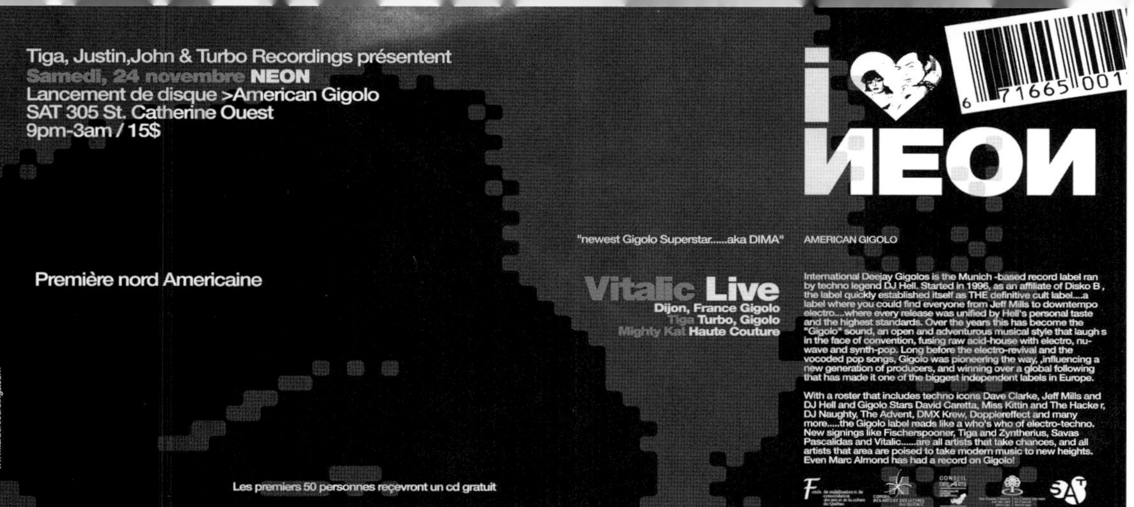
Tiga, Justin,John & Turbo Recordings présentent
Samedi, 24 novembre NEON
Lancement de disque >American Gigolo
SAT 305 St. Catherine Ouest
9pm-3am / 15$
i ♥ NEON
Première nord Americaine
"newest Gigolo Superstar......aka DIMA"
Vitalic Live
Dijon, France Gigolo
Tiga Turbo, Gigolo
Mighty Kat Haute Couture
AMERICAN GIGOLO
International Deejay Gigolos is the Munich -based record label ran by techno legend DJ Hell. Started in 1996, as an affiliate of Disko B , the label quickly established itself as THE definitive cult label....a label where you could find everyone from Jeff Mills to downtempo electro....where every release was unified by Hell's personal taste and the highest standards. Over the years this has become the "Gigolo" sound, an open and adventurous musical style that laugh s in the face of convention, fusing raw acid-house with electro, nu-wave and synth-pop. Long before the electro-revival and the vocoded pop songs, Gigolo was pioneering the way, ,influencing a new generation of producers, and winning over a global following that has made it one of the biggest independent labels in Europe.
With a roster that includes techno icons Dave Clarke, Jeff Mills and DJ Hell and Gigolo Stars David Caretta, Miss Kittin and The Hacke r, DJ Naughty, The Advent, DMX Krew, Dopplereffect and many more.....the Gigolo label reads like a who's who of electro-techno. New signings like Fischerspooner, Tiga and Zyntherius, Savas Pascalidas and Vitalic......are all artists that take chances, and all artists that area are poised to take modern music to new heights. Even Marc Almond has had a record on Gigolo!
www.turborecordings.com
Les premiers 50 personnes reçevront un cd gratuit

electro
NUWAVE
EURO
TRASH
Tiga, Justin,John & Turbo Recordings
Vitalic Live
Dijon, France Gigolo
Tiga Turbo, Gigolo
Mighty Kat Haute Couture
girl

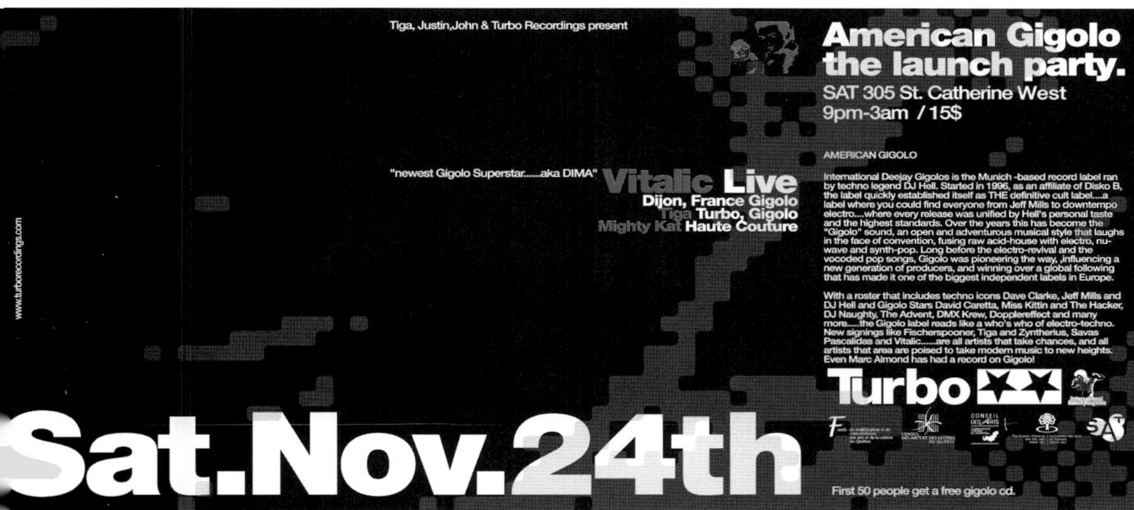
Tiga, Justin,John & Turbo Recordings present
American Gigolo
the launch party.
SAT 305 St. Catherine West
9pm-3am / 15$
"newest Gigolo Superstar......aka DIMA"
Vitalic Live
Dijon, France Gigolo
Tiga Turbo, Gigolo
Mighty Kat Haute Couture
AMERICAN GIGOLO
Turbo
www.turborecordings.com
Sat.Nov.24th
First 50 people get a free gigolo cd.

i ♥
NEON
Samedi, 24 novembre NEON
Lancement de disque >American Gigolo
SAT 305 St. Catherine Ouest
9pm-3am/15$
"newest Gigolo Superstar......aka DIMA"
Première nord Americaine
Vitalic Live
Dijon, France Gigolo
Tiga Turbo, Gigolo
Mighty Kat Haute Couture

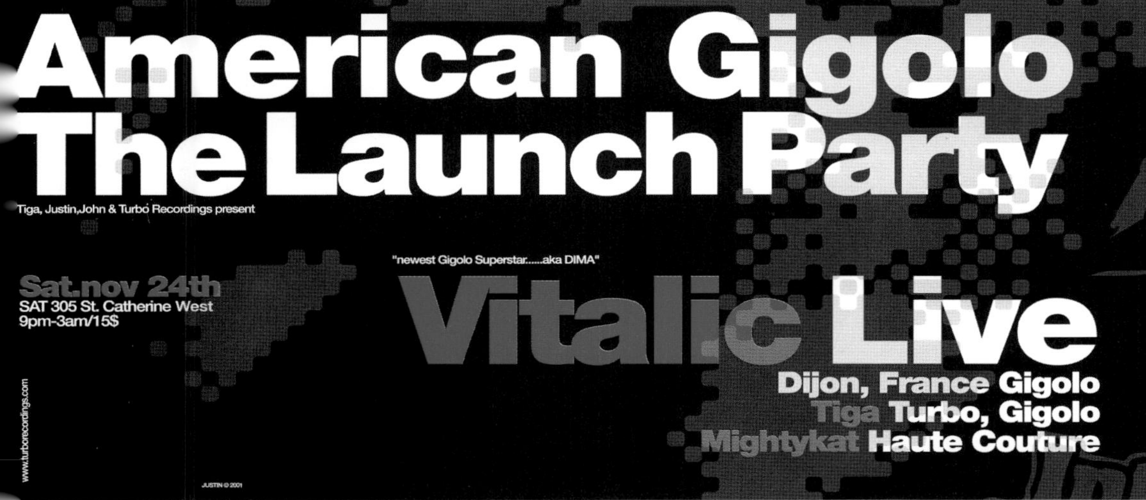
American Gigolo
The Launch Party
Tiga, Justin,John & Turbo Recordings present
"newest Gigolo Superstar......aka DIMA"
Sat.nov 24th
SAT 305 St. Catherine West
9pm-3am/15$
Vitalic Live
Dijon, France Gigolo
Tiga Turbo, Gigolo
Mightykat Haute Couture
www.turborecordings.com
JUSTIN © 2001

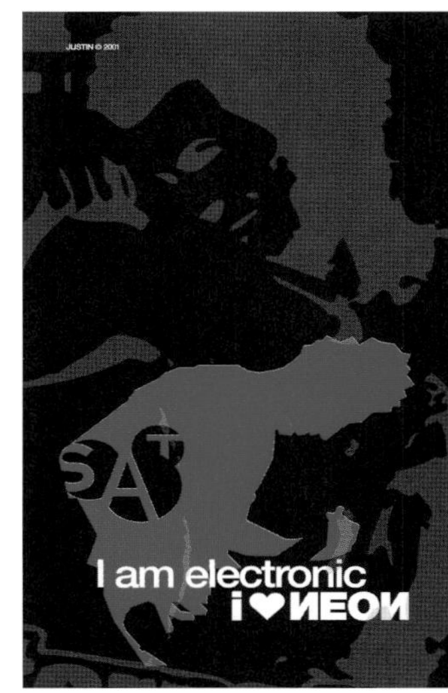
JUSTIN © 2001
I am electronic
i ♥ NEON

NEON ♥ ELECTRO

i am electronik
JUSTIN © 2001

NEON ♥
ELECTRO
fastForward

Dope Brothers
presenta
1er Aniversario
Bongo Lounge
12
jueves

Happening CIBORG

jueves 05 DIMINIC B "STATION WARRIORS" & TAYO Mop records - UK.

viernes 13 AL LINDRUM Lust/Lips - Denmark

jueves 19 RICHARD SEN Bronx Dog - UK

jueves 26 AFRO-LATIN GROOVATHON

Todos los viernes DOPE SESSIONS Latin fussion: Dj+Orchestration

Próximamente en Mayo

sabado 19 SR. COCONUT en concierto

Todos lo jueves apartir de las 12.00h
Todos los viernes apartir de las 2.00 h

Selectors DJ DELIPPO & PROF. ANGEL DUST
Live LA CAMELIA BLANCA
(Mambo, Latin go-go, Bugalú, Latin Soul)
Visuals by ULISSES & PANIAGUA

La Paloma Tigre 27 DownTown Barcelona

Vestax EASTPAK Dewar's "White Label"

Bongo Lounge @ La Paloma | Barcelona | Mariana Sarraute

En estas páginas y las siguientes / These pages and the next
Bongo Lounge @ La Paloma | Barcelona | Mariana Sarraute

5 “3 IS THE MAGIC NUMBER”
dj Carlos LaMar + WilldeLux + Baby G

12 Electrophunkydisco ATTACK!
prof. AngelDust + Baby G
+ Sandro Lustosa (MACACO) percusion

19 BRASILIAN EXTRAVAGANZA
prof. AngelDust + dj deLippo
+ Sandro Lustosa (MACACO) percusion

26 WET LADIES NIGHT
prof. AngelDust +dj deLippo
featuring Danistik (scratch master)
+ Danna Leese (SOUL MAMA)

bailarinas:
Latin Soul Sisters
percussion:
Dominique drum steam

selectors:
Pr. Angel Dust & DeLippo
visuals:
vj Ulysses & vj Paniagua

todos los jueves a partir de las 12.00 pm

La Paloma tigre27, downtown Barcelona

sponsorized by SPUTNIK

8 DB SUPER CLASSICS
dj deLippo & prof. AngelDust

15 BLACK LATIN ROOTS SPECIAL
dj deLippo & WAX GROOVE
(dj Valentin de Moreda + Jeru Aka Ru)

22 COSMIC DISCO NIGHT
dj deLippo & dj Will deLuxe

29 AFRO LATIN FUNK NIGHT
dj Carlos de la Mar & dj Baby G

bailarinas:
Latin Soul Sisters
percussion:
Dominique drum steam

selectors:
Pr. Angel Dust & DeLippo
visuals:
vj Ulysses & vj Paniagua

todos los jueves a partir de las 12.00 pm

La Paloma tigre27, downtown Barcelona

sponsorized by SPUTNIK

Dope Brothers
presenta
Bongo
Lounge

Todos los Jueves apartir de las 12.00h

7 **DOPE BROTHERS' GROOVATHON**
Featuring: MC Ben+Jammin' & Yonder (percusión)

14 **FINGER LICKIN' NIGHT**
Dj Krafty Kuts & Soul of Men

21 **PHAT BEATZ SPECIAL**
Dope Brothers, Dj Caesar, Danistik+guest MC

28 **DOPE BROTHERS**

Selectors **DJ DELIPPO & PROF. ANGEL DUST**

Live **LA CAMELIA BLANCA**
(Mambo, latin go+go, Boogaloo Latin Soul)

Visuals by **ULISSES & PANIAGUA**

La Paloma Tigre 27 DownTown Barcelona

En estas páginas y siguientes / These pages and the next
La Terrazza I Barcelona I Jaime Razquin

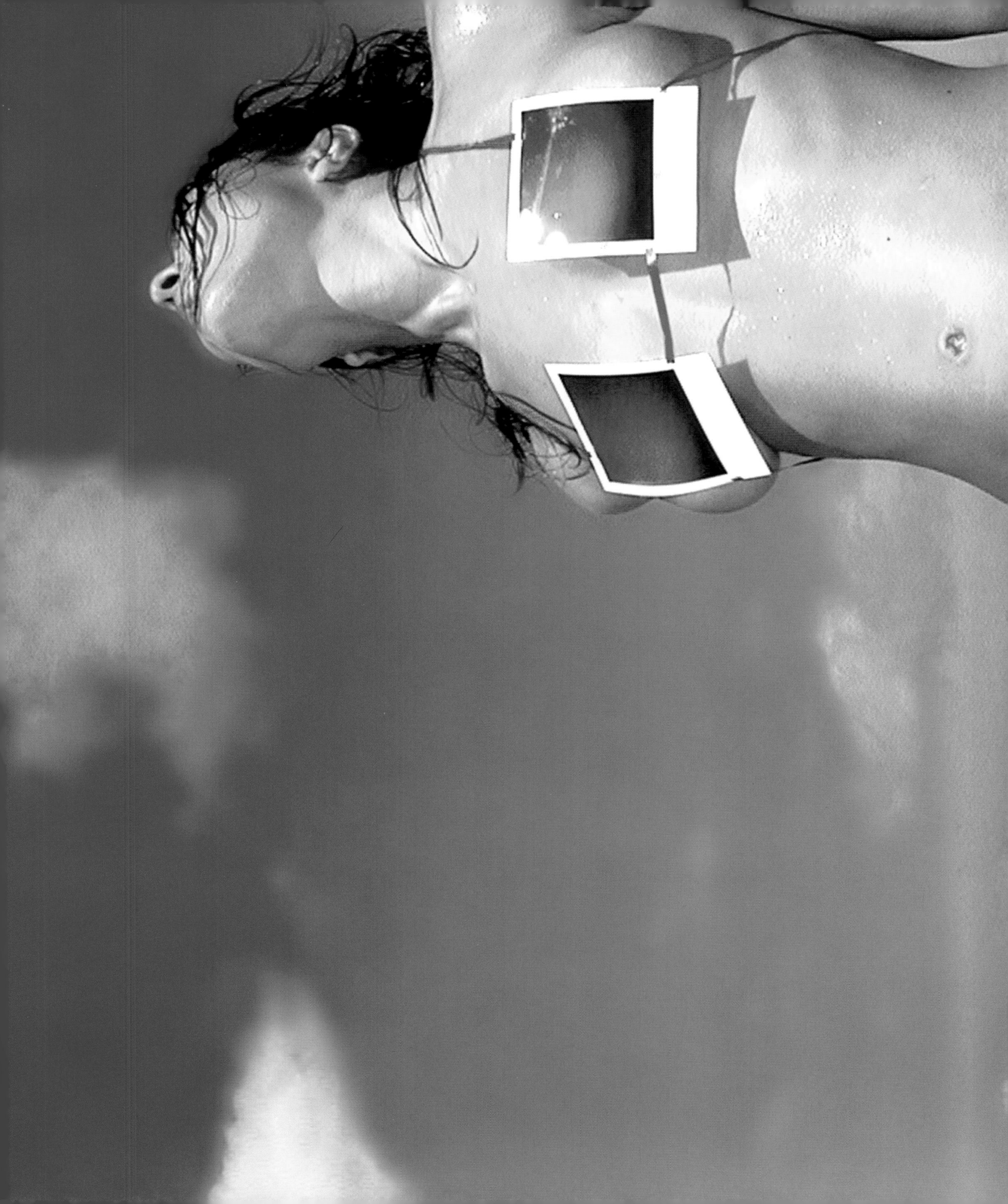

la terrrazza

atmospherical fun club

VOTE
mr. fish

three
ambients
The Bad Room
Free Clash
El Salón de los Espejos
The Bad Room: Room
an open

La fealdad en el soporte gráfico, se puede producir de manera deliberada y consciente. Recogiendo una estética, un lenguaje propio, para utilizarlo en beneficio del eje creativo.

Pero la inconsciencia es la que nos puede dar los resultados más extravagantes, producido por el desconocimiento o el mal gusto del comunicador. Este segundo camino es una puerta abierta a las mentes más aberrantes, donde la imaginación puede llegar a volar a mundos inexplorados.

La escasez de recursos es una característica de la economía de guerra de una parte de estos flyers. El recorta y pega, las fotocopias en papeles de colores. O la reinvindicación cubista de los collages, el montaje sin recursos, la sofisticación del "dimo" y el "letraset". El look fanzinero, la estética punk no ha sucumbido a los dictados de la moda. El mundo underground, lo prohibido, fiestas ilegales, afters, conciertos, presentaciones experimentales, etc, son un caldo de cultivo para estos flyers.

La temática de este discurso puede llegar a ser de lo más variada, otorgando un valor añadido que otros flyers no tienen. Se toman prestados temas e iconos de la televisión, de la cultura pop, del rock, del cine, del sexo... se mezclan entre ellos y aparece: lo extraño, lo anormal, lo kitsch. El delirio puede venir cuando se rapta uno de estos elementos y se coloca en un lugar nuevo, un habitat diferente donde el choque entre ambos crea una nueva "dimensión desconocida" que puede derivar en humor, como arma a su favor, puede ser intencionado (por imagen descontextualizada o por concepto) o por lo que es más divertido: la inconsciencia del autor.

La indiferencia es el mayor fracaso de la comunicación, los mensajes han de impactar, por lo malo o preferiblente por lo bueno. A lo largo de un día estamos expuestos a un sinfín de actos comunicativos y sólo retenemos en nuestro cerebro, un tanto por ciento mínimo.

Los trash flyers por sus características peculiares logran una buena retentiva en las mentes de aquellos que se cruzan en su camino. ¡La eficacia comprobada!

Ugliness in its graphic form can be created deliberately and consciously, representing a style, a language of its own to be used as an aid to creativity itself. The most outlandish results however come from recklessness, produced by the communicator's lack of knowledge or taste. This second route is an open door to the most deviant minds where the imagination is allowed to run riot.

One aspect as regards these flyers is the lack of resources brought on by economic pressures. Cutting and pasting, photocopies on coloured paper or justifiable cubist collages, montage without resources. The fanzine look-alike, punk refusing to succumb to the dictates of fashion! The underground world, the forbidden, the illegal raves, the after parties, the concerts, the original performances, etc... all are a breeding ground for these flyers.

The subject matter of this means of communication can vary to such an extent that it has an added attraction non existent in other flyers. A mixture of icons and topics taken from the worlds of television, pop culture, rock music, cinema and sex come together to create: the strange, the abnormal and the kitsch. Delirium appears when one of these elements is seized and placed in a new and different environment where the clash between the two creates a new "unknown dimension" which might end in humor, a weapon in its favour, whether intentional (by a de-contextualized image or concept) or more agreeably as a result of the creator's reckless abandon.

The biggest hindrance to communication is indifference, the message must make an impact, be it good or bad, though preferably good. We are exposed throughout each day to a never ending barrage of information of which our brains are only able to retain a fraction.

trash flyers on account of their unusual eye-catching features have demonstrated good retentive qualities in the minds of those whose paths they have crossed.

The effectiveness is well proven!

Text by Albert Carreras

Club Fellini | Barcelona | Manel Moedano

SOREBEL! CLUB!
La Paloma
Septiembre

Estilo Propio!
La Paloma
JULIO 2004

La Paloma
agosto 2004
Estilo Propio!
LGH 793

La Paloma
POWER GROOVE
SEPTIEMBRE 2004

La Paloma
WHY NOT?
ABRIL
A. B. SHEPARD
SOREBEL! CLUB!

La Paloma
AGOSTO
SOREBEL! CLUB!

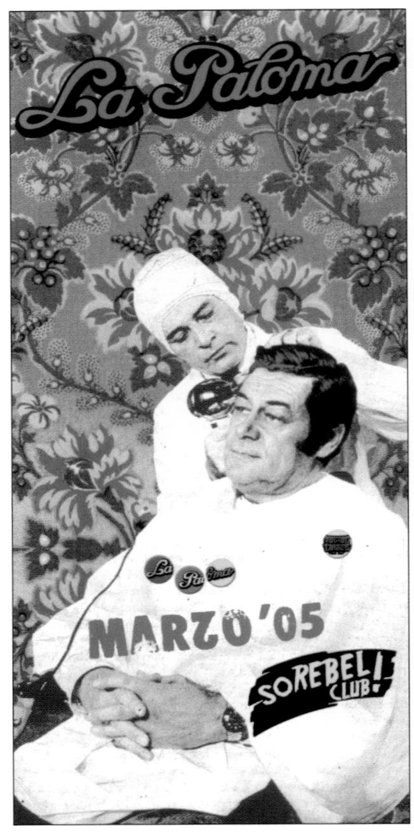
La Paloma
MARZO '05
SOREBEL CLUB!

JULIO
La Paloma
SOREBEL CLUB!

JUNIO 2004
La Paloma
No rules Freestyle!

Octubre
SOULREBEL
La Paloma

JUNIO '05
La Paloma
SOREBEL CLUB!

CHAMPAGNE
No rules Freestyle!
La Paloma
MAYO 2004

La Paloma

SOREBEL! CLUB!
ENERO
2005

CORSO
MOTEL
OPEN
QUEENS DOUBLES
KITCHENETTES
CORSO
CORSO
CORSO
CORSO

MERRY CHRISTMAS
CORSO
HAPPY BIRTHDAY MASCOTTE
1 YEAR
CORSO
CORSO
PARK MASCOTTE
ENTRANCE
CORSO
CORSO

Night Sun Group presenta
club
FELLINI
del 16 al 19 de Junio 2005
SONAR WEEKEND
Jueves 16 Sábado 18
SONAR WEEKEND
Viernes 17 Domingo 19
Jueves 16 de Junio
ALBERTO R. & MISS ERIKA
Viernes 17 de Junio
MARIO MAQUEDA
Sábado 18 de Junio
PELUCAS & FREDERIC
Domingo 19 de Junio - Sonar Alter Party
DJ HELL

Night Sun Group presenta
club
FELLINI

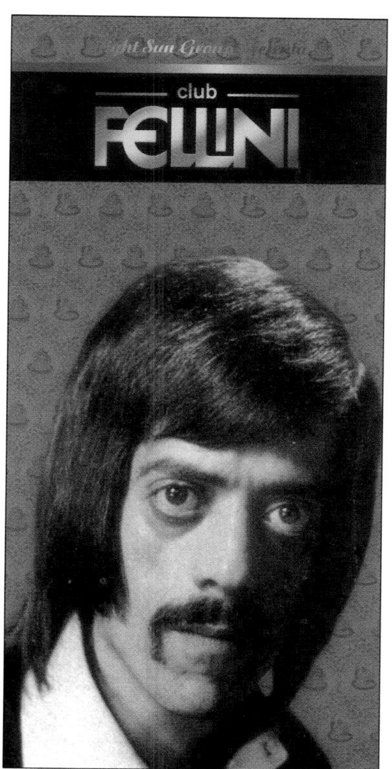
club
FELLINI

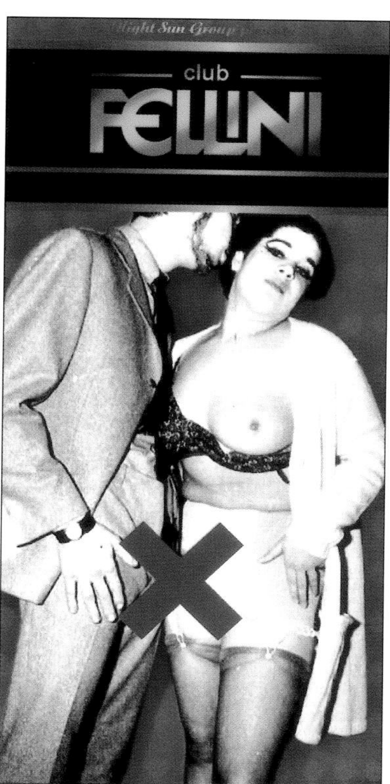
club
FELLINI

club
FELLINI
three ambients
3€
El Salón de los Espejos
The Bad Room
The Red Room
club
FELLINI

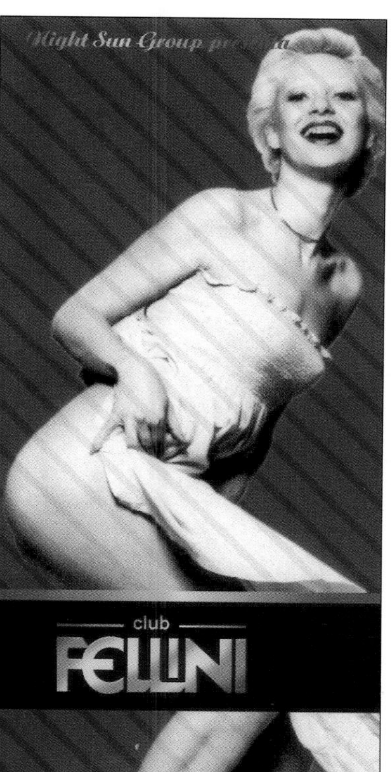
club
FELLINI

club
FELLINI
Entrada gratuita!*
CARNAVAL VENEZIANO
Baile de Máscaras

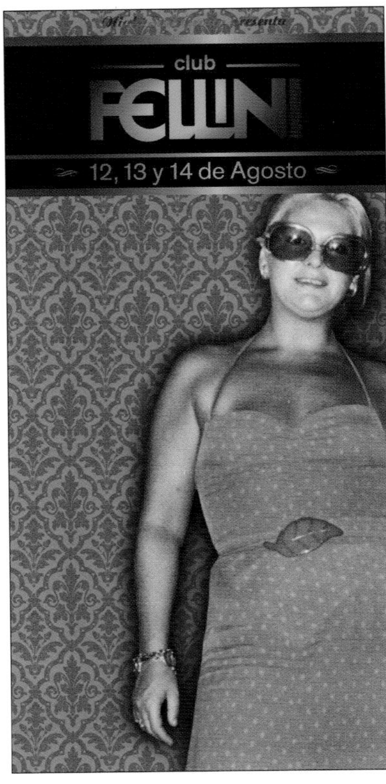
club
FELLINI
12, 13 y 14 de Agosto

Night Sun Group presenta
club
FELLINI
CARNABALL DISCO
Baile de Disfraces

Night Sun Group presenta
club
FELLINI
26 y 27 de Marzo

club
FELLINI
29 y 30 de Abril

club
FELLINI
23 y 24 de Septiembre

club
FELLINI
22 y 23 de Julio

club
FELLINI
6 y 7 de Mayo

club
FELLINI
Chic House, Free Clash, Nu Disco
MARTES 6 DE SEPTIEMBRE
In da Ghetto
free

club
FELLINI
8 y 9 de Abril

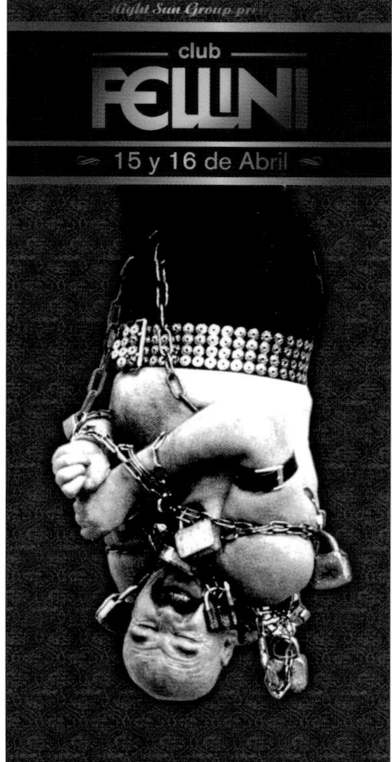
club
FELLINI
15 y 16 de Abril

club
FELLINI
20 y 21 de Mayo

club
FELLINI
24 y 25 de Junio

Mond Club | Barcelona | Sergio Ibáñez

MOND
BAR

MOND
BAR

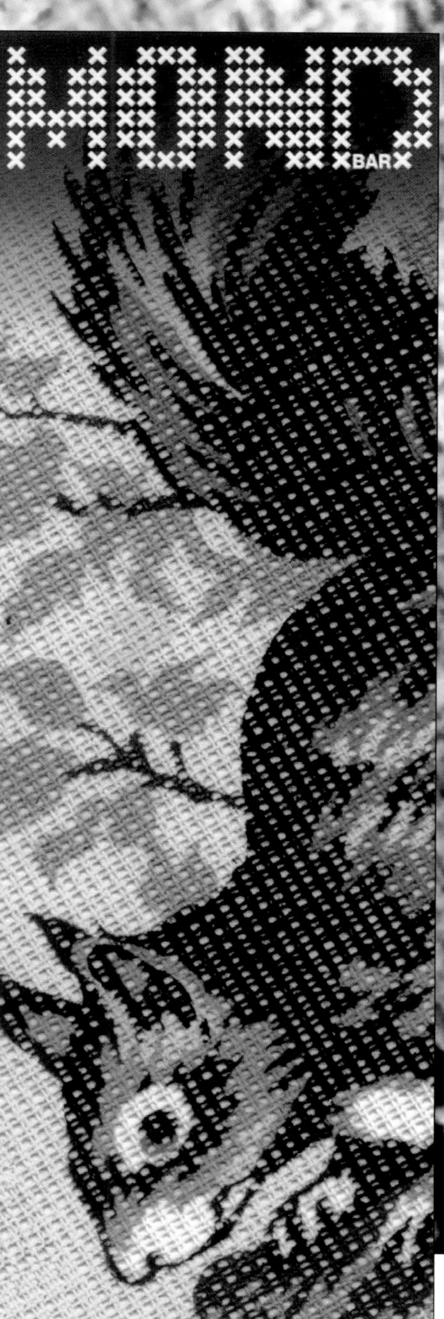
MOND
BAR

Le Noveau Casino I Paris I Grégoire Dalle

Le Noveau Casino | Paris | Grégoire Dalle

La Scene Bastille | Paris | Grégoire Dalle

A la Scène bastille on écoute Radio Nova
nova
PRÉFÉRENCES
La Scène Bastille
LA SCÈNE BASTILLE
WWW.LA-SCENE.COM
2, BIS RUE DES TAILLANDIERS 75011 PARIS
TÉL: 01 48 06 50 10 = FAX: 01 48 06 57 01
2 bis rue des Taillandiers
METRO BASTILLE
RESTAURANT LA SCÈNE BASTILLE
Du mardi au samedi, de 19h30 à Minuit
N° Tel Réservations Restaurant : 01 48 06 12 13
WOMBAT
tyler
PROGRAMMATION
Juin
La Scène Bastille
2 bis rue des Taillandiers
METRO BASTILLE

BEACON
HOTEL
POLICE
Miami

DIS COTH EQUE
KEN
Presents
WEDNESDAY MARCH 10th 2004
The best club in BARCELONA at
Miami Winter Music Conference
all night long from 11pm till 5am at
CROBAR VIP ROOM
with the Djs
BOB SINCLAR
(Yellow Productions / Mona Rennalls Agency)
DJ PIPPI
(Ibiza / Mona Rennalls Agency)
PIERRE RAVAN
(Spiritual Brothers / Mona Renalls Agency)
LEE STARK
(Ken Pachá Ibiza / Discothèque Barcelona)
BONNIE PARKER
(Barcelona)
and live performances
BARBARA TUCKER & LUCA G.
in collaboration with
MADE IN ITALY
IBIZA
ibiza 04
CROBAR MAIN ROOM
with the Djs
RALF & ALEX NERI
(Planet Funk / Serial Killer Vinyl)
Midnight Fashion Show
JUST CAVALLI
hosted by
ROCCO ANCAROLA
crobar
1445 Washington Avenue
Ph: 305.531.8225 Table reservations: 305.531.5027
www.crobarmiami.com www.helice.info www.madeinitalyibiza.com
Miami
HELICE MANAGEMENT
PROPAGANDA MUSIC
YELLOW PRODUCTIONS
TEN YEARS OF MUSIC
mona.rennalls.agency
www.mona-rennalls.de
artwork:
www.tonicolomar.com
ALL STARS
DJs Festival

Discothèque | Barcelona | Toni Colomar
CDLC Lounge Club & Restaurant | Barcelona | cdlcbarcelona.com

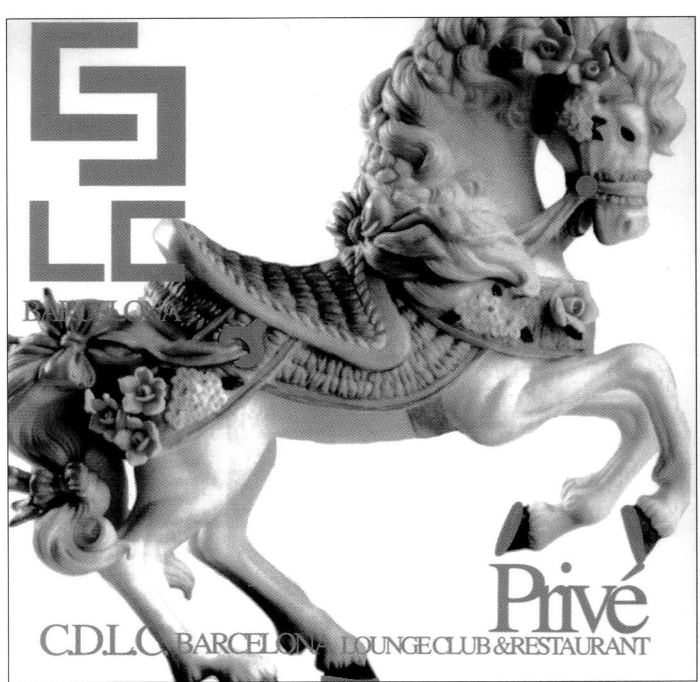

SIROCO
WANTED
dj´s Residentes sala SIROCO:
GUDLAK & JJ BERNARDO
C/ San Dimas 3 - <M> NOVICIADO
Jueves, Viernes y Sabados 00:30 a 06:00 $
www.siroco.es

SALVATION
GAY DISCO
presenta a:
TAMARA
presentado su disco "No Cambié"
ACOMPAÑADA POR SU MAMA, MARGARITA SEISDEDOS...
EN EXCLUSIVA PARA EL PUBLICO GAY
VIERNES NOCHE 15 DICIEMBRE
el sol sale igual para todos
MATINÉE GROUP
presenta
le soleil
après la nuit
DJ MIKEL MOLINA
DJ ERIK
Pº Marítimo de la Barceloneta, 36
(entrada por la playa)

Siroco | Madrid | Chop
Salvation | Barcelona | Neus Cardona
Le Soleil | Barcelona | Neus Cardona

Los Miércoles en Fellini
Stairway to heaven!!
MIÉRCOLES / WEDNESDAY
Beat Connection
ACID HOUSE :: TRASH DISCO :: PUNK FUNK
CLUB FELLINI • LAS RAMBLAS 27 • BARCELONA

rex club
Dirty
Playing
JEUDI 30 OCTOBRE
A PARTIR DE 23H30
ENTRÉE LIBRE
MISSIVE
Joe Tex

diciembre 2002

2003
THESE EYES
God Made Me Hardcord

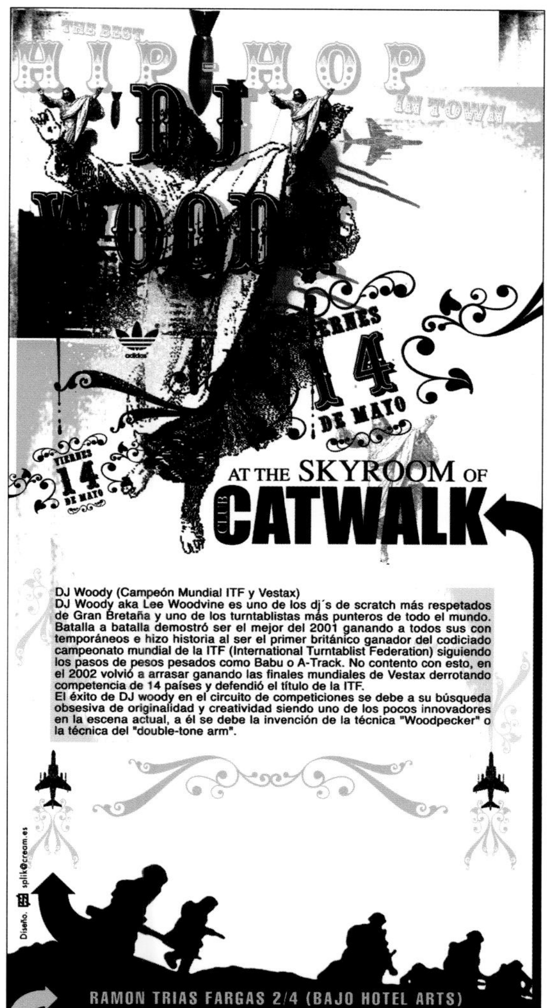

THE BEST
HIP-HOP
IN TOWN
DJ
WOODY
VIERNES
14
DE MAYO
AT THE SKYROOM OF
CLUB CATWALK
DJ Woody (Campeón Mundial ITF y Vestax)
DJ Woody aka Lee Woodvine es uno de los dj´s de scratch más respetados de Gran Bretaña y uno de los turntablistas más punteros de todo el mundo. Batalla a batalla demostró ser el mejor del 2001 ganando a todos sus con temporáneos e hizo historia al ser el primer británico ganador del codiciado campeonato mundial de la ITF (International Turntablist Federation) siguiendo los pasos de pesos pesados como Babu o A-Track. No contento con esto, en el 2002 volvió a arrasar ganando las finales mundiales de Vestax derrotando competencia de 14 países y defendió el título de la ITF.
El éxito de DJ woody en el circuito de competiciones se debe a su búsqueda obsesiva de originalidad y creatividad siendo uno de los pocos innovadores en la escena actual, a él se debe la invención de la técnica "Woodpecker" o la técnica del "double-tone arm".
Diseño. splik@creom.es
RAMON TRIAS FARGAS 2/4 (BAJO HOTEL ARTS)

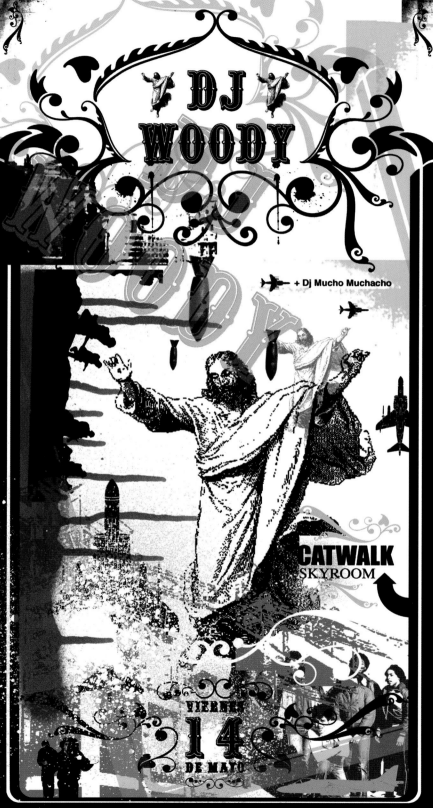

DJ
WOODY
+ Dj Mucho Muchacho
CATWALK
SKYROOM
VIERNES
14
DE MAYO

Página izquierda / Left page
Club Fellini | Barcelona | Manel Moedano
Rex Club | Paris | Grégoire Dalle
Bongo Lounge @ La Paloma | Barcelona | Mariana Sarraute
Risco | Barcelona | Brothers in love
En esta página / This page
Club Catwalk | Barcelona | Splik

En esta página / This page
Decadance | Ibiza | Álvaro Villarrubia
Página derecha / Next page
La Troya Asesina | Ibiza | Álvaro Villarrubia

Dope Brothers
海
煙
東
華
中
Bongo Lounge
Septiembre 2002

Lesya Starr
presenta
danza y música oriental
Fiebre Oriental!
Jueves 11 de Julio
entre 22.00 y 24.00 hrs.
La Paloma Tigre 27.Barcelona
entrada: 8 euros ★ info: 93 317 79 94

Dope Brothers
presentan
Bongo Lounge
abril 04

Dope Brothers
Bongo Lounge
MARZO★02

Dope Brothers
Bongo Lounge
FEBRERO 02

Dope Brothers
presentan
Bongo Lounge
julio 04

Dope Brothers
presentan
Bongo Lounge
junio04

Dope Brothers
Enero 2003
Bongo Lounge

Bongo Lounge
Julio 2003
Dope Brothers

Dope Brothers
presenta
Bongo Lounge
Julio 2001
La Paloma Tigre 27 DownTown Barcelona

Dope Brothers
DOPE BROTHERS
Bongo Lounge
enero★02
d

Dope Brothers
Bongo Lounge
noviembre 04

Dope Brothers
presentan
the sound is back!
Bongo Lounge
febrero'04

Dope Brothers
4º Aniversario
Bongo Lounge
mayo 04

Dope Brothers
presentan
Bongo Lounge
marzo 05

Dope Brothers
marzo'03
Bongo Lounge

Dope Brothers
The sound is coming!!!
Bongo Lounge
enero 04

Dope Brothers
Bongo Lounge
agosto-02

Bongo Lounge
Noviembre 2003

Dope Brothers
PRESENTAN
BEST FRIEND
BEST FRIEND
Bongo Lounge
ENERO 05

ELECTRONIC . HOUSE . CLUB

ARTWORK BY: WWW.TONICOLOMAR.COM

...is **different**

Enero 2004

viernes y sábados

Dj residents:

Eric Morin & bubu

viernes 23

fiesta **Catedral**

Dj **Abraam** y **Victor**

Arquitecto Moragas 28.
El Prat de Llobregat.Barcelona

Viernes todo a 3€.

Sábados chicas entrada libre.

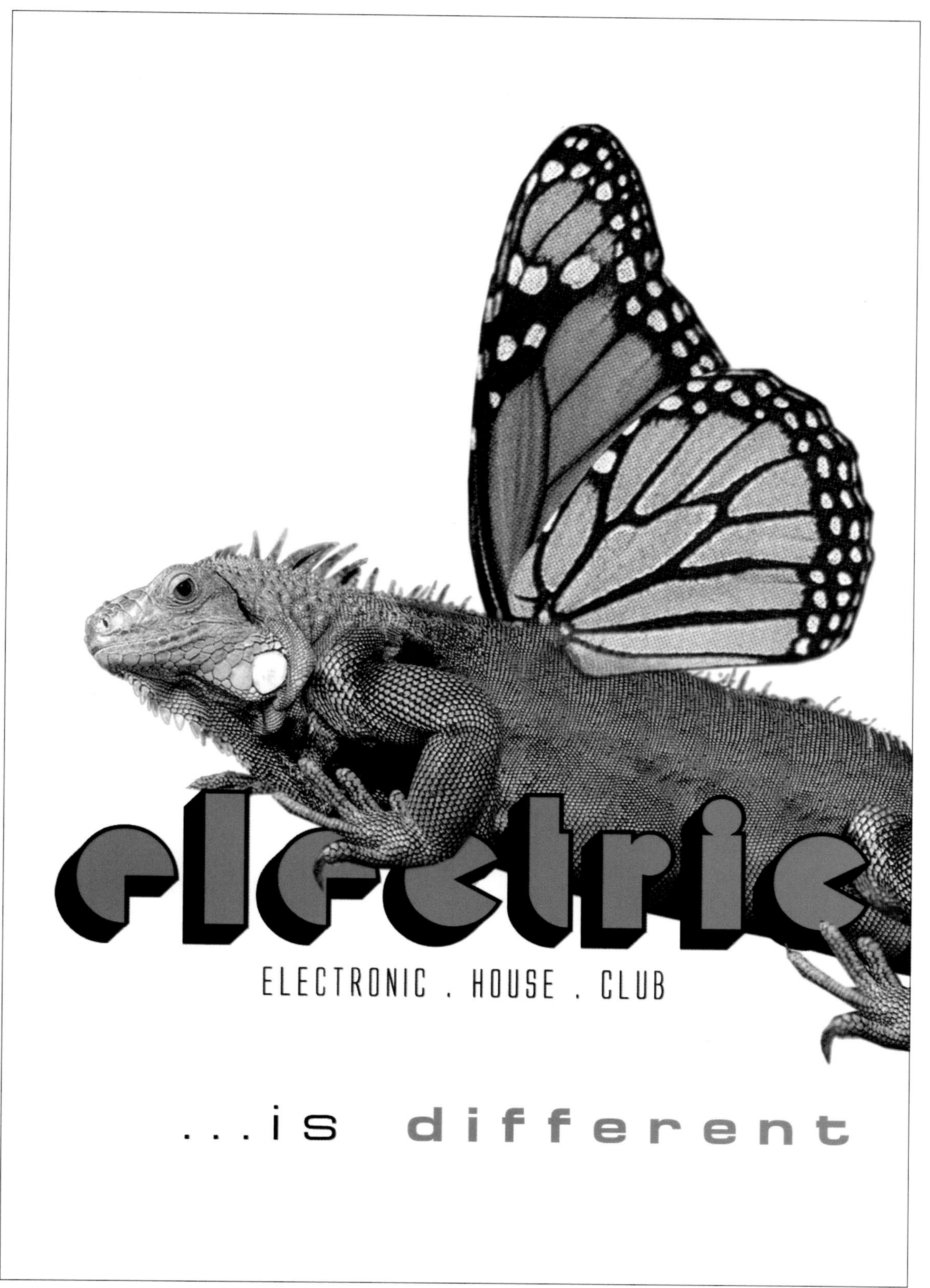

Electric | Barcelona | Toni Colomar

love FIG

Freak Bar | Barcelona | Sr.Mr.Lou
The Cock | London | ghetto-london.co.uk

SEX PORNOCHIC

El Sexo ha pasado de ser un tabú a introducirse de manera inadvertida, casi sin darnos cuenta en nuestro día a día, como algo habitual de lo que no escandalizarse o avergonzarse. Muchos diseñadores utilizan iconos e imágenes relacionados con el mundo del sexo, en muchas ocasiones de manera tan explícita que hace que el mensaje pueda ser malinterpretado por aquellas personas que carecen de cierta sensibilidad artística. El sexo está de moda: sexo en la televisión, sexo en los video-clips, sexo en las escuelas, sexo en los periódicos, sexo en las pasarelas, sexo en las revistas de moda, sexo, sexo, sexo... La pornografía de los años setenta, aquella que marcó época por su atrevimiento al tratar el sexo como algo de lo más común entre los seres humanos, ha sido rescatada para crear un nuevo estilo, una mezcla de moda, diseño y sexo, un movimiento que algunos denominan "pornosoft" o "pornochic". Órganos sexuales, tanto masculinos como femeninos, lucen todo su esplendor en ilustraciones e imágenes que más que excitarnos provocan una sonrisa de oreja a oreja. Con la llegada de la libertad de expresión, llega la libertad sexual y a su vez la libertad en la forma de diseñar.
Dejando prejuicios a un lado nos encontramos frente a una nueva era plástica.

Almost without our realising, sex has gone from being treated very much as a taboo subject to introducing itself in an impartial manner into our everyday lives, as something habitual which neither scandalises nor causes embarrassment. Many designers use icons and images related to the world of sex, in many cases explicit enough for the message to be misinterpreted by those who lack a certain degree of artistic perception. Sex is in vogue: sex on television, sex in video-clips, sex in schools, sex in the newspapers, sex on the catwalks, sex in fashion magazines, sex, sex, sex....
The pornography of the seventies, a time marked by its daring for treating sex as something common between human beings, has been salvaged to create a new style, a mix of fashion, design and sex, a movement which could be known as "pornosoft" or "pornochic". Sexual organs both masculine and feminine are displayed in all their glory in the form of illustrations and images and which rather than arouse us are more likely to provoke a smile from ear to ear. With the arrival of freedom of speech, came sexual freedom and at the same time freedom in the form of design.
Leaving prejudices aside we find ourselves in the presence of a new plastic era.

MAKE DESIGN NOT WAR!

Discothèque | Barcelona | nightsungroup.com
Gay T Dance @ Apolo | Barcelona | Álvaro Villarrubia

DICIEMBRE DE 2002
D1. LE FREELANCE
L2. DJ OH!
M3. KÄRLEK DJ
X4. URI CALLEJO
J5. READY, STEADY, BAR! PALOMA & BUENAVISTA
V6. MIQUI PUIG
S7. B-SIDES
D8. GODEO
L9. SUITE DJS
M10. VALLE
X11. UNFINISHED
J12. READY, STEADY, BAR! PEY
V13. FELICIDADBLANCH (LIVE!) + UN COCACOLA
S14. NIÑO
D15. OLIVA DJ
L16. GABI & VIO
M17. ONE SIAMISS
X18. FANNY & MANDELBAUN
J19. READY, STEADY, BAR! ENEIDA FEVER
V20. SCHOOLDISCO AT THE BAR! LAS PERRAS DJS
S21. PEP MUNUERA
D22. PRINGUI DJ
L23. MR DJ
M24. JINGLE JINGLE METRALLETA: BONNIE & CLYDE
X25. KILIAN
J26. READY, STEADY, BAR! VESPAPINCHADISCOS
V27. NO DJ
S28. SIDONIE DJS
D29. JAIME CASAS
L30. JACKSON FIORE
M31. FIN DE AÑO: WELCOME 2003 WITH BONNIE & CLYDE
San Miguel, donde está tu música
MOND BAR
POP WILL MAKE US FREE
PLAÇA DEL SOL, 21 BARCELONA
ABIERTO CADA DIA A PARTIR DE LAS 20.00H.
INFO: 93.272.09.10 WWW.MONDCLUB.COM
San Miguel
MOND BAR
POP WILL MAKE US FREE
PLAÇA DEL SOL, 21 BARCELONA
MOND BAR
POP WILL MAKE US FREE
PLAÇA DEL SOL, 21 BARCELONA
MOND BAR
POP WILL MAKE US FREE
PLAÇA DEL SOL, 21 BARCELONA

NOVIEMBRE
ESTACION DE FRANCIA
FIGHT
republica
underthestation

republica
underthestation
INVITACION x2

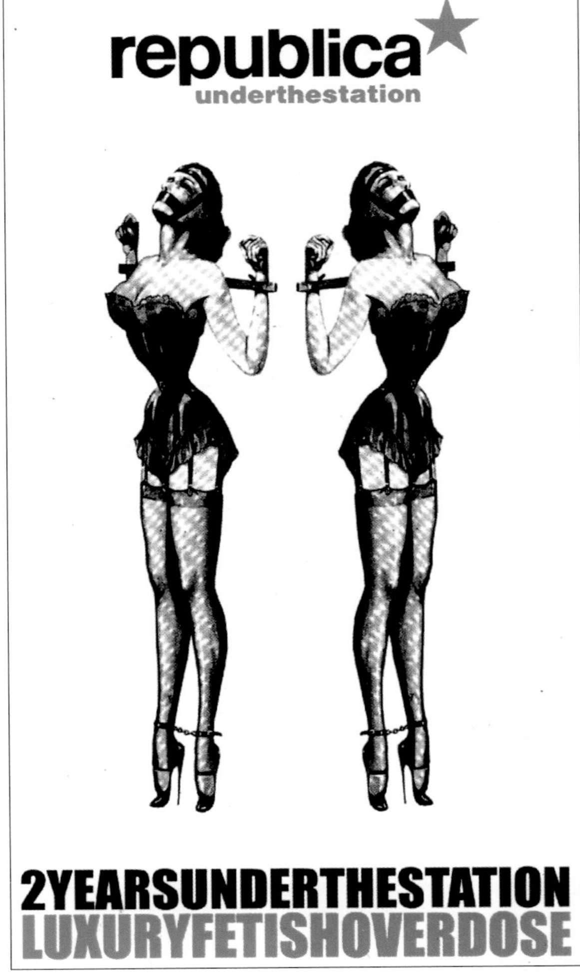
republica
underthestation
2YEARSUNDERTHESTATION
LUXURYFETISHOVERDOSE

republica
underthestation
MUSIC
NATION

Club Catwalk | Barcelona | Oscar Cardó

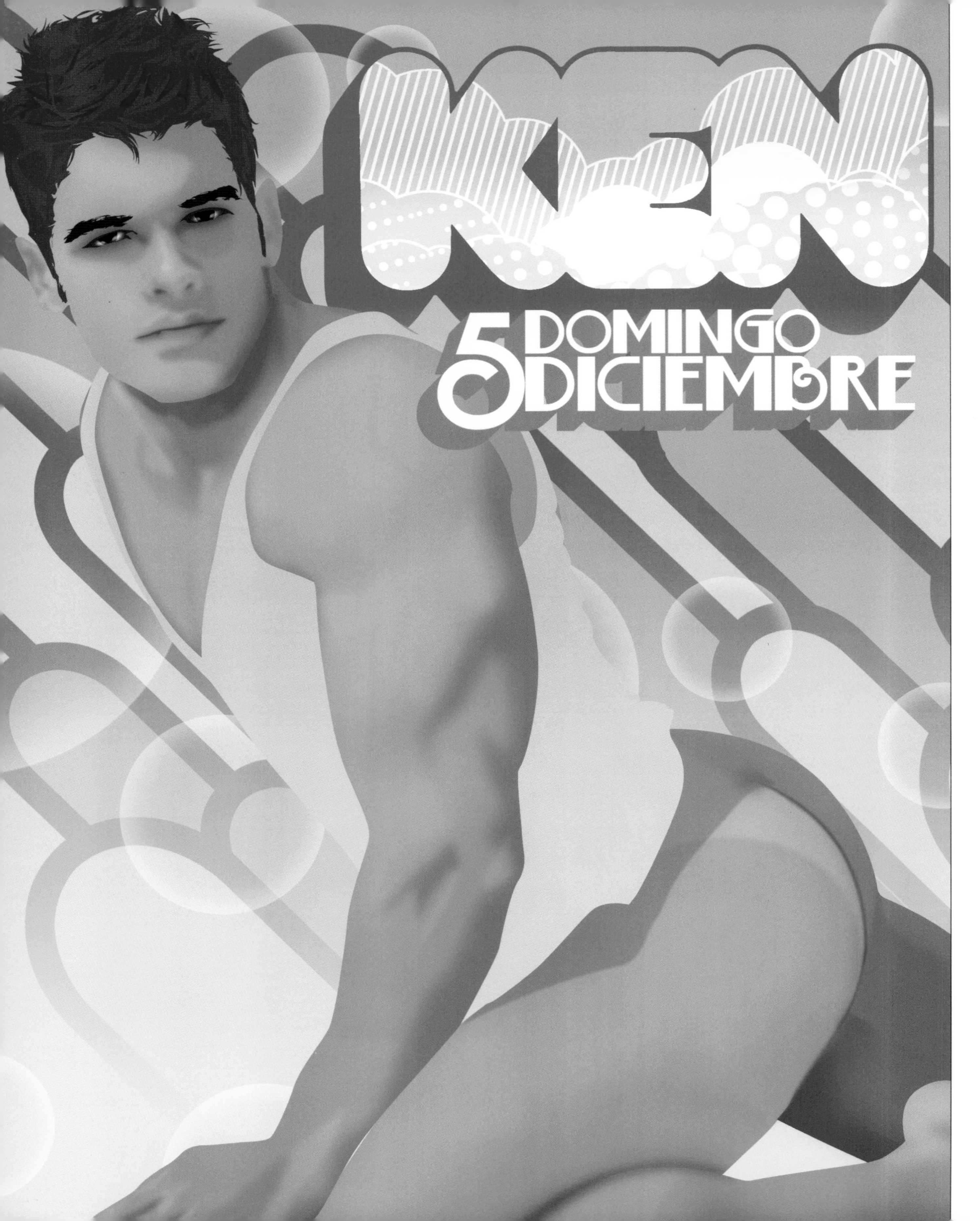
KEN
5 DOMINGO
DICIEMBRE

who loves you?

TOP RATED

KEN LOVES YOU!™

KEN

siempre activo

love power

Saturday
November 1st
with music by
PACO CARRO (soultronic)

plus: Ken's lovers,
more than go-go's, they are actually beautiful human beings

poble espanyol de barcelona

DIS
COTH
EQUE

VICTOR

Colorola BARCELONA

En estas páginas / On these pages
Discothèque | Barcelona | Stuart Patterson

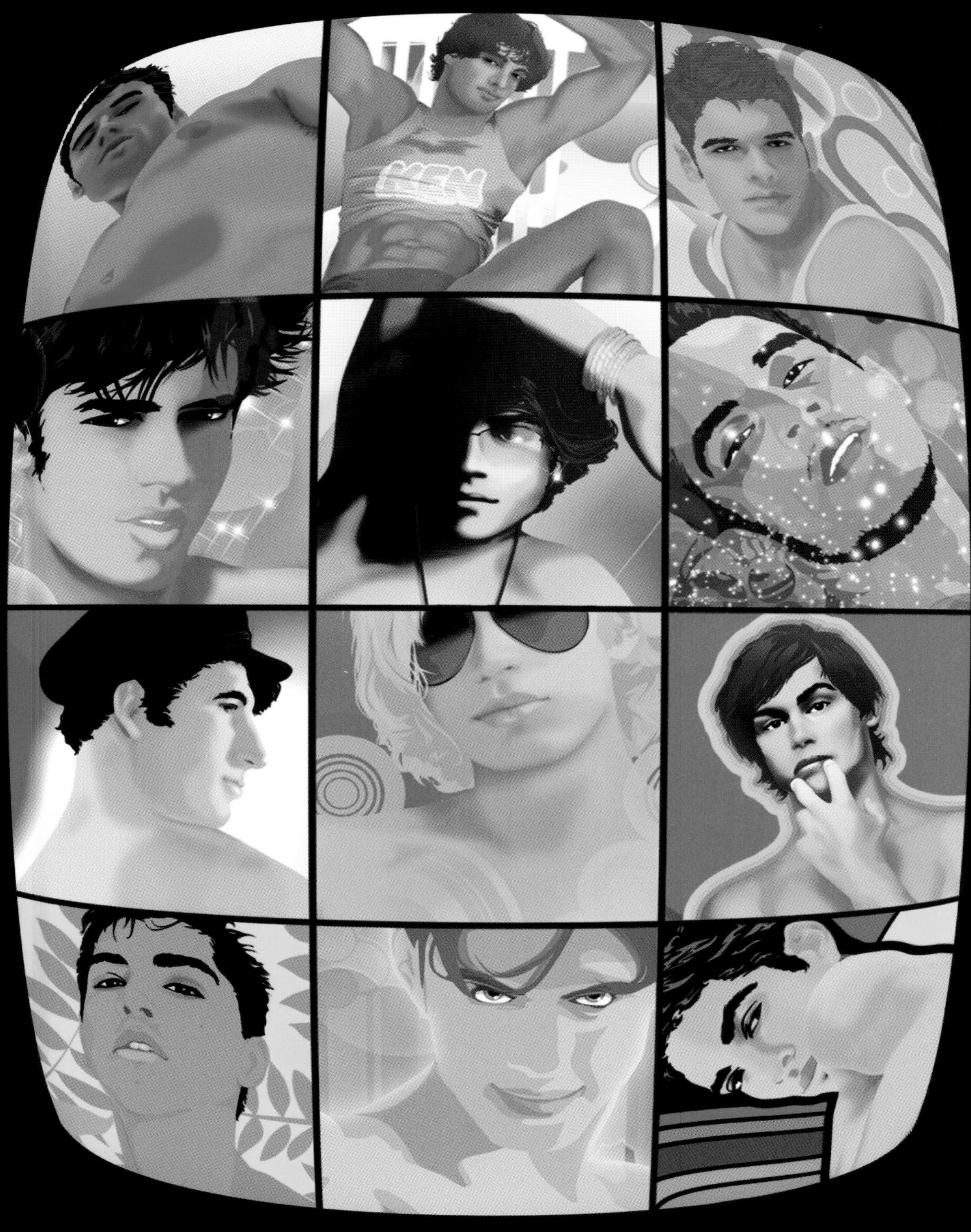

The men of Ken

03.12.05.BARCELONA

New York Club | Barcelona

SEXPLOSION#1
Sexplosion
#6
VIERNES
7
MAYO
la fiesta gay
más dura del mes
¿PODRAS
AGUANTARLO?
SALVATION
gay disco
INVITACION
ENTRADA
HASTA LAS
3:15h
colabora:
PASES
RDA SANT PERE 19-21. BARCELONA. MATINEEGROUP.COM

Página izquierda / Left page
Pacha Ibiza | Ibiza | Álvaro Villarrubia
En esta página / This page
Gay Tea Dance @ Apolo | Barcelona | Álvaro Villarrubia

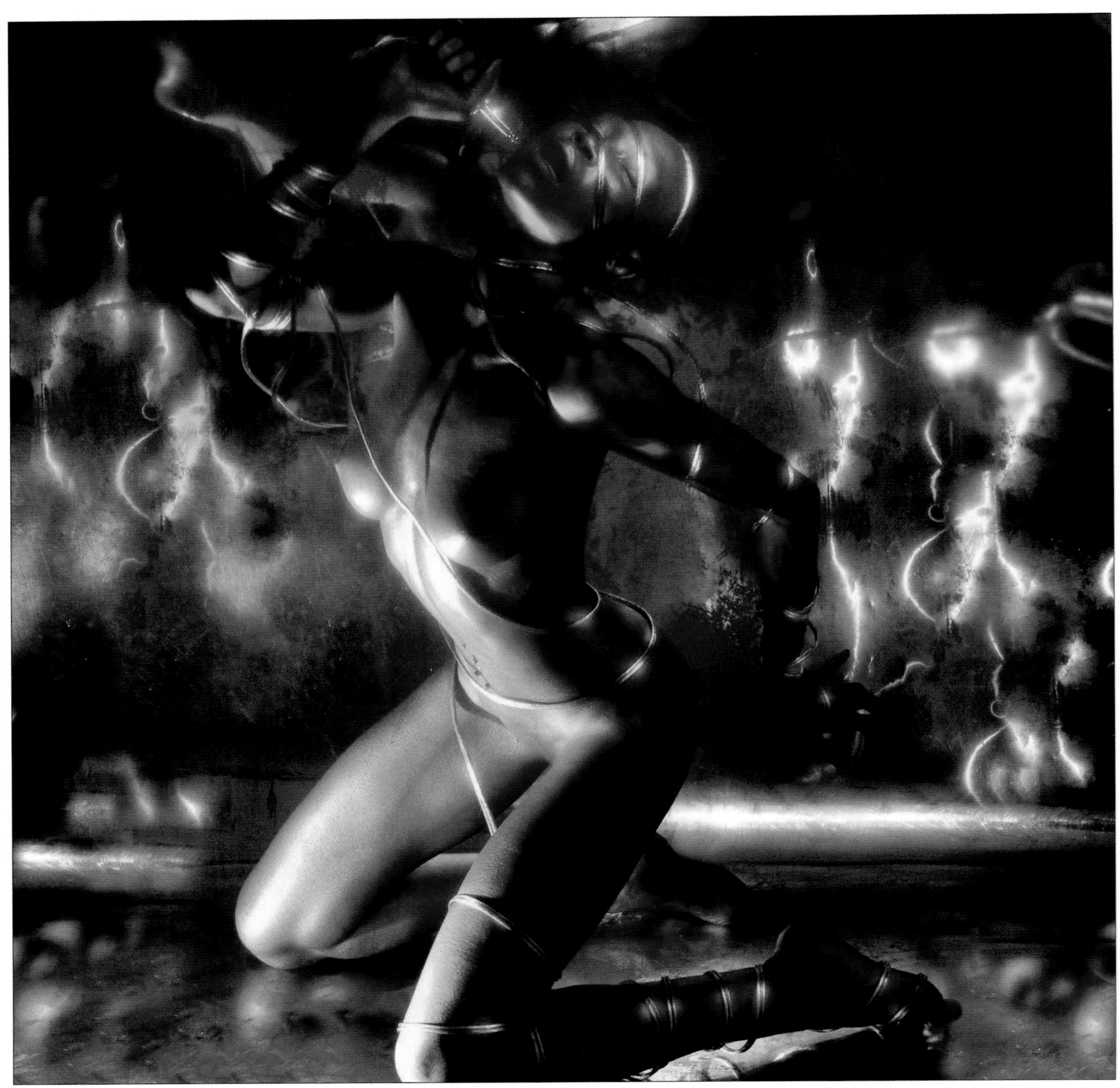

Discothèque | Barcelona | Javier Pardo
Discothèque | Barcelona | Toni Colomar
Club Danzatoria | Barcelona | clubcatwalk.net

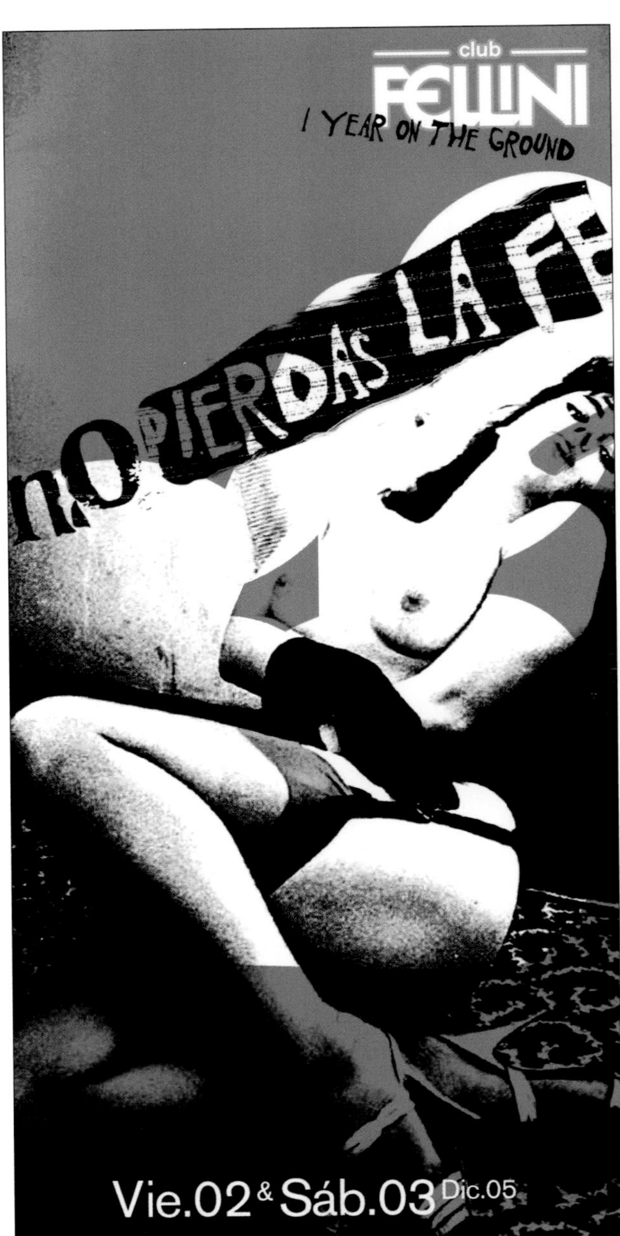

Club Fellini | Barcelona | Manel Moedano

club
FELLINI
esta en nuestra naturaleza
Viernes.04 & Sábado.05 Nov.05
Sábado 05 Nov.05
Salón de los Espejos
Indigo:
Vincenzo & Minus Love
The Bad Room
Mario Maqueda (Fellini)
The Red Room
Ragnampaisser
(somosunekipo.com)
(Fellini)
BIOGRAPHICS DE
Club Fellini · Las Ramblas 27
Open from Wednesday to

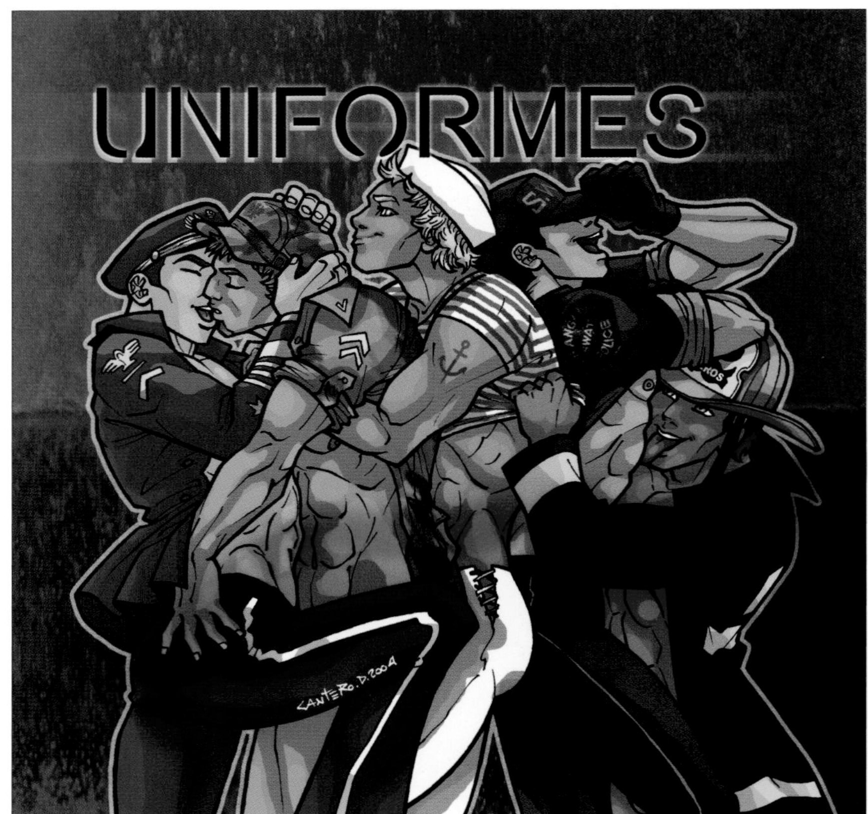

En esta página / This page
Gay Day @ Space | Barcelona | David Cantero
Trade | Ibiza | tradeuk.net
Club Ohm | Madrid | Iván Soldo
Freak Bar | Barcelona | Sr.Mr.Lou

Freak bar

DISCOTHEQUE
ALWAYS WITH YOU!!
DEVOTION
HOT DOG

wwW.nagnagnag.inFo
naG Nag nAg

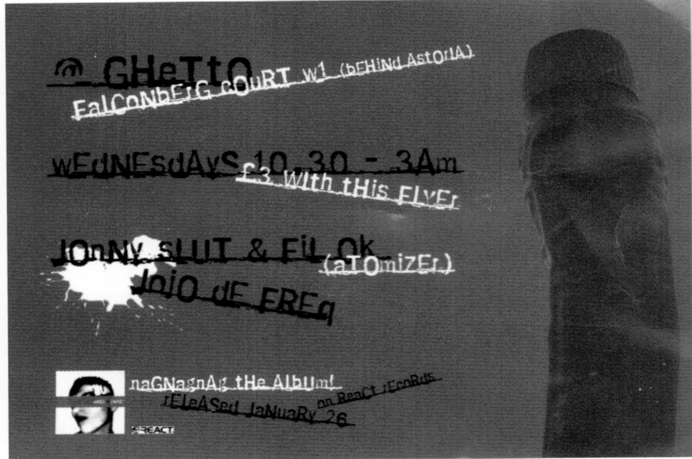
@ GHeTtO
FalCoNbErG cOuRT w1 (bEHiNd AstOrIA)
wEdNEsdAyS 10.30 - 3Am
£3 With tHis FLyEr
JOnNY SLUT & FiL Ok (aTOmizEr)
JoJO dE FREq
naGNagnAg tHe AlbUm! on ReAct rEcoRdS
rEleASed JaNuaRy 26
REACT

Discothèque | Barcelona | Toni Colomar
Dos Trece | Barcelona
Dirty Dancing | Belgium | Luis Arenas

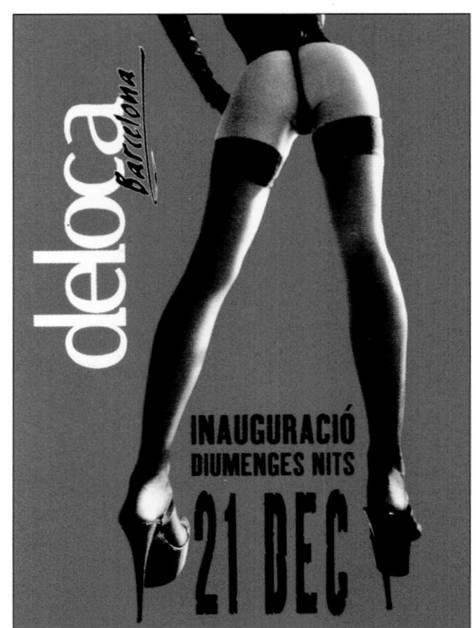

KISS

bettyboop club

Donde la diva perdió su inocencia...

01.01.2004

bettyboop club

En esta página / This page
Deloca | Barcelona | delocadanceclub.com
Kiss | Barcelona
Rimmel Club | Barcelona
Betty Boop Club | Barcelona
Discothèque | Barcelona | Toni Colomar
Página derecha / Right page
Acapulco | Zurich | Nadine Geissbühler

ACAPULCO
proudly presents:
BURLESQUE
Night
especially for you
THE
VELVET HAMMER
SHOW
from Los Angeles
THU. 4TH DEC. '03, 10 PM
MUSIC BY:
Dj Grau
"The point is not to strip but to tease."
15.-
Entry
Acapulco
TEASERAMA

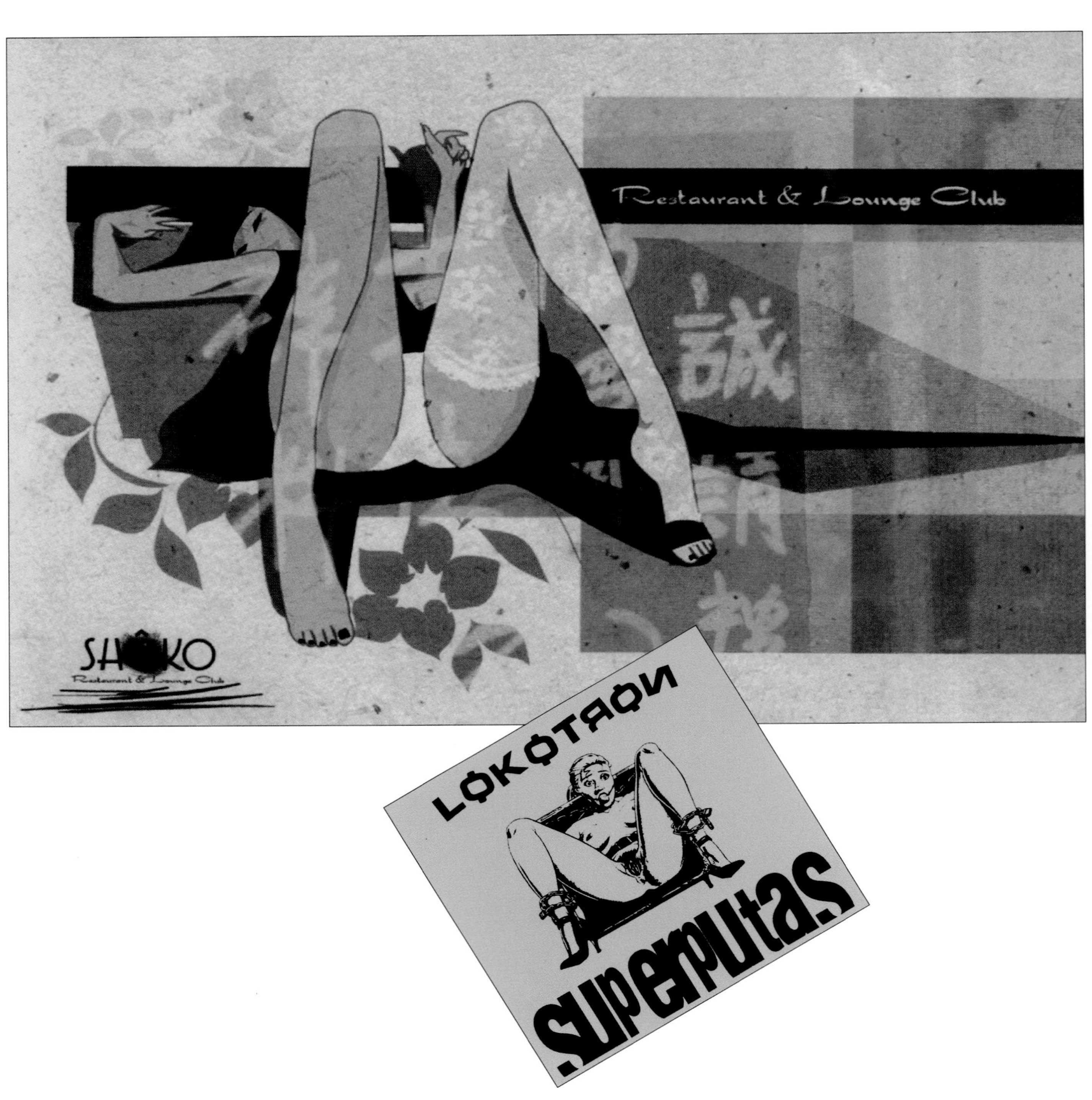

Shôko restaurant and lounge club | Barcelona | Oscar Cardó
Lokotron | Barcelona | lokotron.com

PORNOGRAPHY

OR ART?

Erotica underground party | Barcelona
Nitsa Club | Barcelona | nitsa.com

duri
30 YEARS OF
SCRATCHY TOP HITS
FRIDAY 13th.
AT 11 pm. SHARP
CLUB
DEL MAR
Tallers 45
(entrant
pel passatge
al fons a
l'esquerra)
DJ Pepe
'7 Wheels'
SURF PARTY
(Surf-Frat-Combo)
with THE WALKYSONS

Regreso al pasado

La temática y estilos retro se ha convertido en un motivo muy utilizado en los flyers de última generación. No hay nada más efectivo que recurrir a imágenes y estéticas del pasado para remarcar la actualidad de una fiesta y otros eventos culturales. Se podría decir que al igual que en el arte establecido en la creación de flyers tampoco se ha inventado nada nuevo y que también se produce el todo vuelve: clasicismo, decó, vanguardia, dadaísmo, pop, punk, con todos los neos y posts que se quieran añadir.
Estos flyers son el espejo del momento presente y la mirada minuciosa o superficial al arte y la cultura del pasado. El uso de tipologías e iconografías pretéritas, copiando indiscriminadamente si es necesario, es otro de los caminos que toma el flyer en búsqueda de una forma de expresión propia.

Retro themes and designs have come to be used extensively in the latest generation flyers. There is, it seems, nothing more effective than resorting to images and styles from the past to draw attention to present day festivities and cultural events. It might be said there's nothing new in the type of art used to create flyers and that likewise everything produced will come back in time: classicism, art deco, avant-garde, Dadaism, pop, punk, including all the neo and post periods as you would like to add.
These flyers not only reflect the moment in time but provide us with a glimpse, albeit detailed or superficial, of art and culture from the past. In search of its own form of expression, the flyer also makes use of past typologies and iconographies, in some cases copied rather indiscriminately.

En estas páginas / On these pages
Club del mar I Barcelona I Jordi Duró
The other place I Barcelona I Jordi Duró
Shotwell I Barcelona I Jordi Duró
Barbar Ann I Barcelona I Jordi Duró

Now available at your planet :
SPACE GRITS
SPACE GRITS
KUNG-FOO

UNIQUE CLUB & SMIRNOFF IMPORTED VODKA PRESENT
SMIRNOFF
CLUB VIEW
DJ SWAMP!
(BECK-DJ / USA)
FREITAG,
23. MARZ
UNIQUE
BOLKERSTRASSE 30
DÜSSELDORF-ALTST.
support DJs:
Henry Storch
Gunar Ruschak

UNIQUE 1999
PROGRAMM
JANUAR `99

En esta página / This page
Bongo Lounge | Barcelona | Mariana Sarraute
Siroco | Madrid | Chop
Unique Club | Düsseldorf | Frank Pop
Mascotte | Zurich | Nadine Geissbühler
Página izquierda / Left page
Unique Club | Düsseldorf | Frank Pop

Nuit des électrons libres | Paris | Grégoire Dalle
Club Mascotte | Zurich | Nadine Geissbühler

FRIDAY 19TH
NOVEMBER '04
10 PM
LET US
ENTERTAIN
YOU
STRICTLY DRESSCODE!
FOR MEMBERS & FRIENDS ONLY
Shake your Ace, Break some Beats,
Bang your Heads & Stomp your Feet!

ZOUK / PHUTURE ADMISSION
PRICING
BEFORE 10PM
AFTER 10PM
27 MAY
$12
$20 / $25
$15
$23
$28
28 MAY
$12
$20
$25
$15
$23 / $28
03 JUNE
$12
$20 / $25
$15
$23
$28
04 JUNE
$12
$20 / $25
$15
$23
$28
incl. 2 std drinks
ADDRESS
17 JIAK KIM STREET
SINGAPORE 169420
PHONE
+65 6738 2988
WEB
ZOUKCLUB.COM
+ ZRMX.COM
THE Clubber's GUIDE TO THE WEEKEND
DON'T PANIC!
ZOUK
Friday
03.06.05
+++++ ZOUK +++++
HED KANDI WITH
TOM DE NEEF (HOLLAND) &
JACK MCCORD (AUSTRALIA)
+++++ PHUTURE +++++
FLAVA WITH
ANDREW CHOW
+++++ VELVET UNDERGROUND +++++
JEREMY BOON
+++++ WINE BAR +++++
TONY TAY
Saturday
04.06.05
+++++ ZOUK +++++
LEE BURRIDGE '365' TOUR (UK)
+++++ PHUTURE +++++
PHUTURE BREAKS WITH
TONY TAY
+++++ VELVET UNDERGROUND +++++
BRENDON P
+++++ WINE BAR +++++
ANDREW CHOW
Hed Kandi with
TOM DE NEEF
& JACK MCCORD
Formed in 1999 by DJ and A&R man Mark Doyle, Hed Kandi is a lifestyle concept incorporating a record label, a radio show, international club nights and a graphic style that stimulates all the senses. Unique and distinctive, Hed Kandi has become a staple of quality, a benchmark by which all compilations are judged. A sophisticated addition to any CD collection, Hed Kandi is music for anyone who has lost them self on a dance floor. This tour welcomes Dutch house hero Tom de Neef who's high profile remixes for the likes of Kylie Minogue, Roger Sanchez, Kings Of Tomorrow and ATFC, plus appearances on several Hed Kandi compilations, have sealed Tom's position in the Kandi team. Joining him will be another long time touring resident for the label – Jack McCord from Australia.
hed kandi
CHIVAS REGAL 12

En estas páginas / On these pages
Shake it up! Sessions | Barcelona | Jordi Duró
En las páginas siguientes / Next pages
The Boiler | Barcelona | Jordi Duró

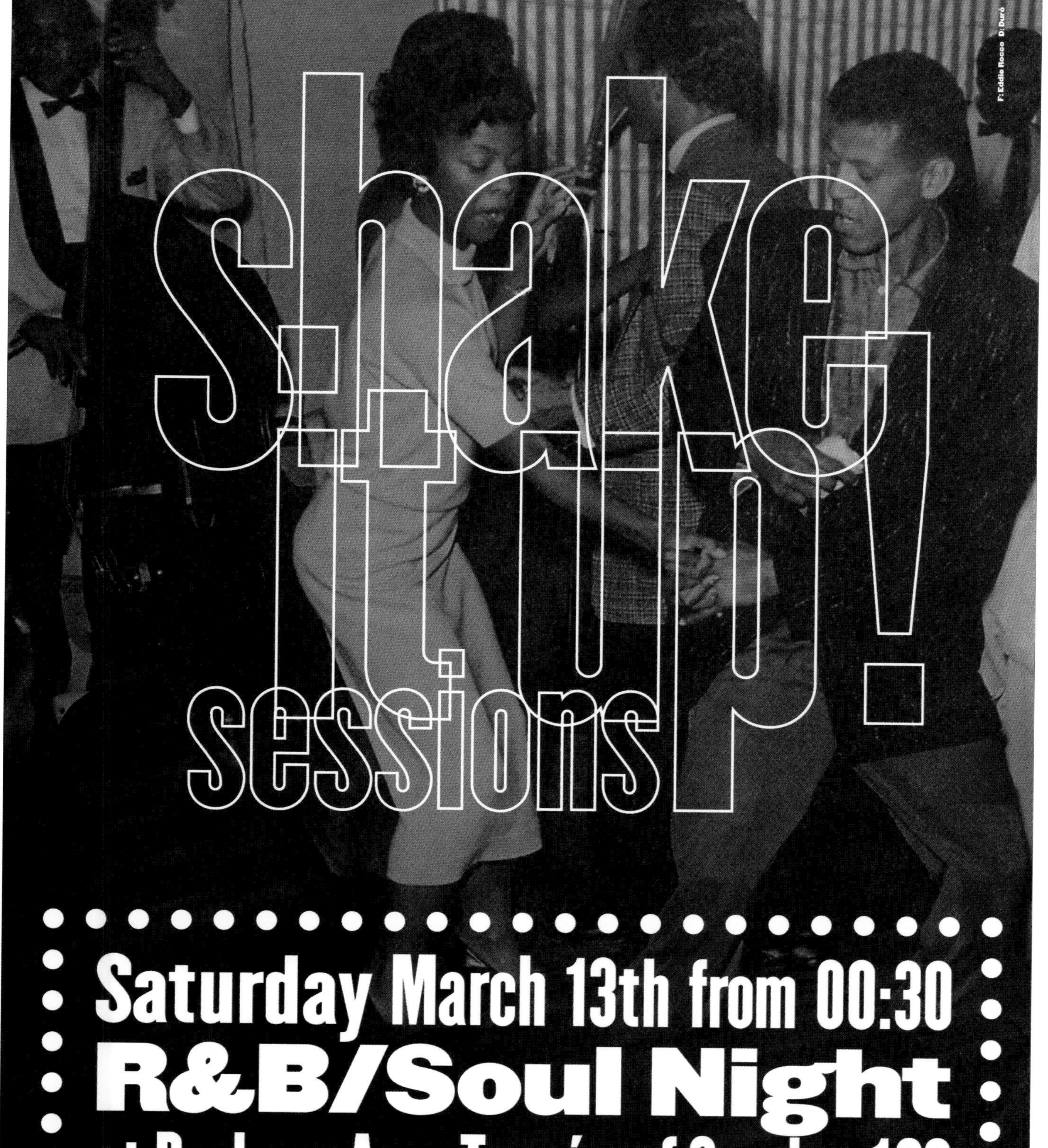

Saturday March 13th from 00:30

R&B/Soul Night

at Barbara Ann, Taquígraf Garriga 163

DJ's: Cristina Alonso + Jordi Duró

D: Jordi Duró F: Eddie Rocco

the Boiler

Rhythm and Soul Club

Friday November 12th

from 24:00 until 5:00

5 euros

Guest DJs:

Paula Obaya

Tarragona

Eddie Hope

London

Resident DJs:

Cristina Alonso

Jordi Duró

Juan Ibáñez

Sala Frank Dubé

Carrer Buscarons 18

Barcelona

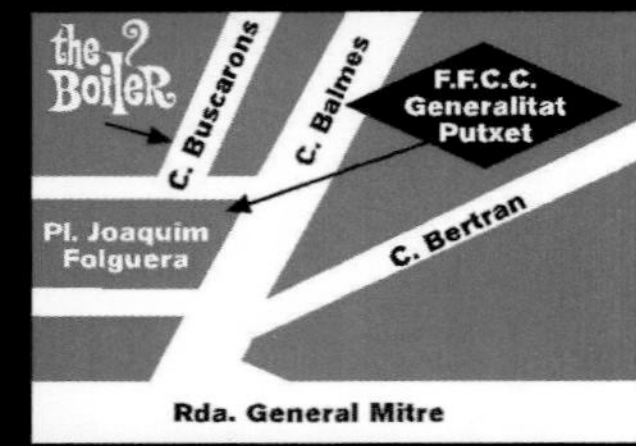

D: Jordi Duró F: Unknown (Clyde McPhatter)

the Boiler

Rhythm and Soul Club
Saturday January 15th
from 24:00 until 5:00
5 euros

Guest DJs:
Sergio Martínez
Madrid
Frantic Al
Barcelona

Resident DJs:
Cristina Alonso
Jordi Duró
Juan Ibáñez

Sala Frank Dubé
Carrer Buscarons 18
Barcelona

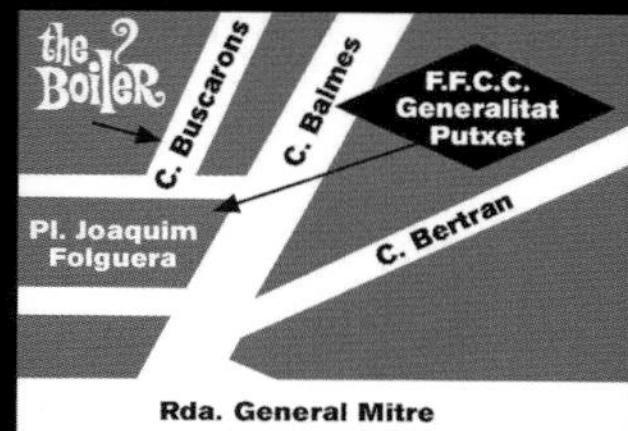

UNIQUE
MÄRZ 99

STEREO
THE DYNAMIC SOUL SOUND OF THE
SUGARMAN THREE
UNIQUE
"SWEET SPOT"
EUROPEAN TOUR 2001

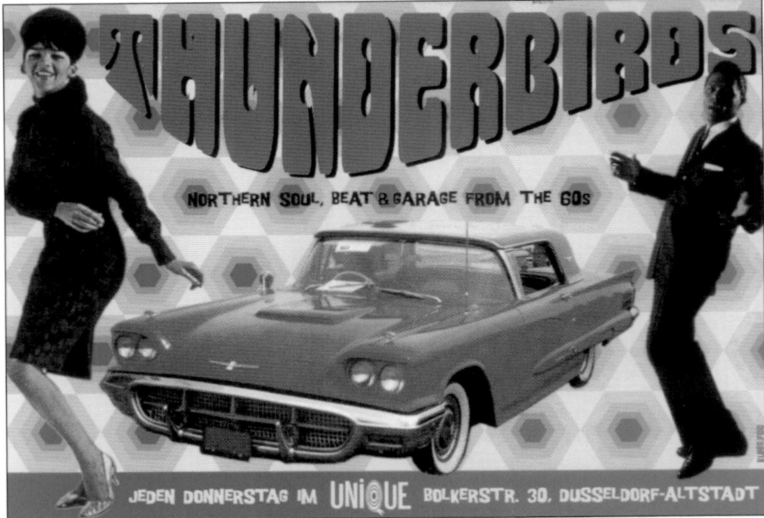
THUNDERBIRDS
NORTHERN SOUL, BEAT & GARAGE FROM THE 60s
JEDEN DONNERSTAG IM UNIQUE BOLKERSTR. 30, DUSSELDORF-ALTSTADT

THUNDERBIRDS
THE SIXTIES FREAKOUT
WHERE THE ACTION IS...
NORTHERN SOUL, BEAT, R&B & GARAGE
BY DJs & LIVE BANDS.
EVERY THURSDAY AT THE
UNIQUE CLUB

UNIQUE
OKTOBER 99
50

FRANK POPP & HENRY STORCH
introduce
SUPERSOUND
a soul, funk & beat review
19.3. 16.4
um 21.00 uhr im unique, bolkerstr. 30, d.dorf-altstadt

Jueves 27 de Febrero 00.30h.
Telephunken
Dj Set
C/SAN DIMAS 3
Metro: Noviciado. Tlf:915933070
Www.siroco.es
SIROCO
Entrada Libre, Invitacion a Segunda Copa con este Flyer

Invitación valida hasta completar el aforo
SOBRINUS
Jueves 18 de diciembre, 21'30h
Fiesta presentación Nuevo Disco de... SOBRINUS
"13 Muecas compiladas" + Sobrinus Dj's
ENTRADA LIBRE - GRATIS - FREE!!!
desofa
sobrinus 13 muecas compiladas
SIROCO
C/San Dimas 3
www.siroco.es

Saturday February 12th from 00:00
FURIOUS FEMALES
(shake it up! 1st anniversary)
at Barbara Ann, Taquígraf Garriga 163
Lavern Baker
(Georgette Duró)
Wynona Carr
(Lady Diana)
Etta James
(Eva Aller)
Tina Turner
(Cristina Alonso)
Ruth Brown
(Frantic Alberta)
One Drink: One Vote
D: Duró

Viernes 1 de Agosto, 22:00h.
CALAMIDAD
GARCIA
C/SAN DIMAS 3
PRECIO ENTRADA CONCIERTO: 5 EUROS
Operación BIKINI

THE WIPEOUT WEEKEND

The surf-beat-r'n'b-garage festival

May 8th, 9th & 10th 2003
Calella, Costa del Maresme,
Barcelona. Spain.

Página izquierda / Left page
The Wipeout Weekend Festival | Barcelona | Jordi Duró
En esta página / This page
Screamin' Festival | Barcelona | Jordi Duró

En estas páginas / These pages
Zouk Club | Singapore | Jim

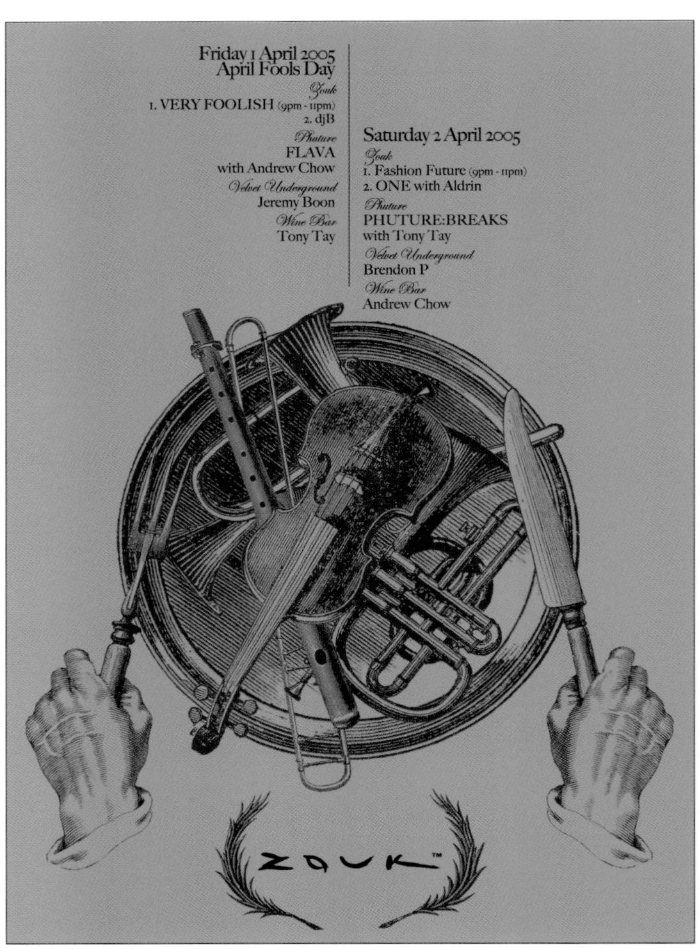

Friday 1 April 2005
April Fools Day
Zouk
1. VERY FOOLISH (9pm - 11pm)
2. djB
Phuture
FLAVA
with Andrew Chow
Velvet Underground
Jeremy Boon
Wine Bar
Tony Tay
Saturday 2 April 2005
Zouk
1. Fashion Future (9pm - 11pm)
2. ONE with Aldrin
Phuture
PHUTURE:BREAKS
with Tony Tay
Velvet Underground
Brendon P
Wine Bar
Andrew Chow
ZOUK™

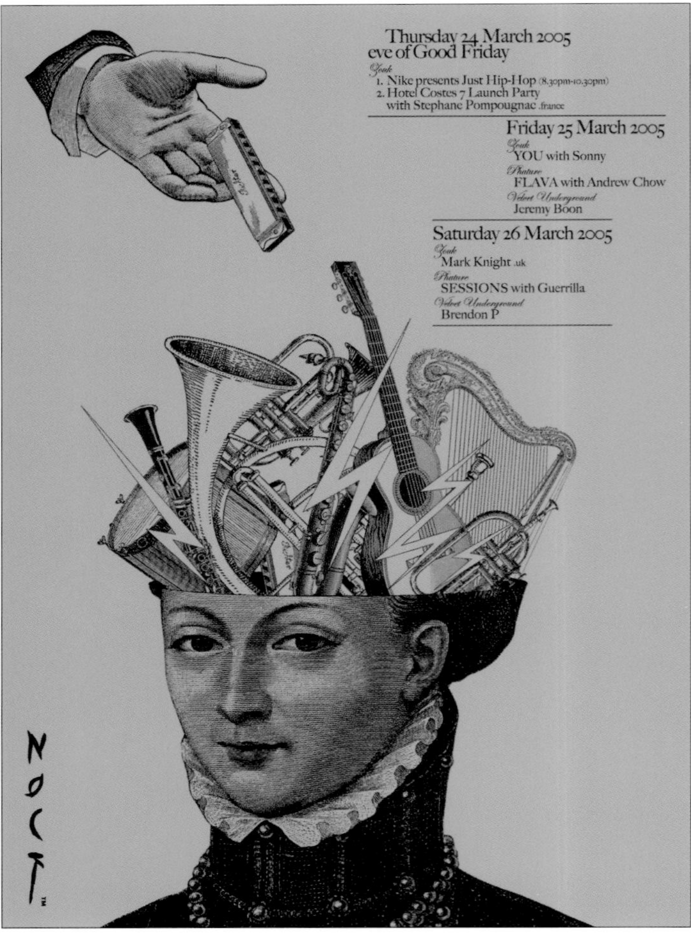

Thursday 24 March 2005
eve of Good Friday
Zouk
1. Nike presents Just Hip-Hop (8.30pm-10.30pm)
2. Hotel Costes 7 Launch Party
with Stephane Pompougnac .france
Friday 25 March 2005
Zouk
YOU with Sonny
Phuture
FLAVA with Andrew Chow
Velvet Underground
Jeremy Boon
Saturday 26 March 2005
Zouk
Mark Knight .uk
Phuture
SESSIONS with Guerrilla
Velvet Underground
Brendon P
ZOUK™

ZOUK™
IT'S
ALIVE!

FLY IV
LA TROYA ASESINA
SE VA A
LA PRISION
amnesia
TERRAZA COCO-LOCO (LA AUTÉNTICA)
MIERCOLES
WEDNESDAY 1 AGOSTO
ELECTROSPLASH
6-10 AGOSTO 2004
RICARDO VILLALOBOS
PANTYTEC
TONY MASS
THE SAINT
GRATIS/FREE
WWW.ELECTROSPLASH.COM
THE LOFT
VIERNES 14
tiga
(DJ KICKS TOUR) + Undo
OMAR
(MINIFUNK/BCN)
WWW.THELOFTCLUB.COM
I AM RISCO
HMS TRADE
LOKOTRON
Pin up's
PACHA BARCELONA
circoloco ibiza
PACHA
LONDRES
VIERNES 30 ENE
JAY JAY
JOHANSON DJ
& HAZCASO
NakedMusic presenta
una noche en el jardín de las delicias...
WWW.NITSA.COM

FLYERS FLYERS FLYERS...

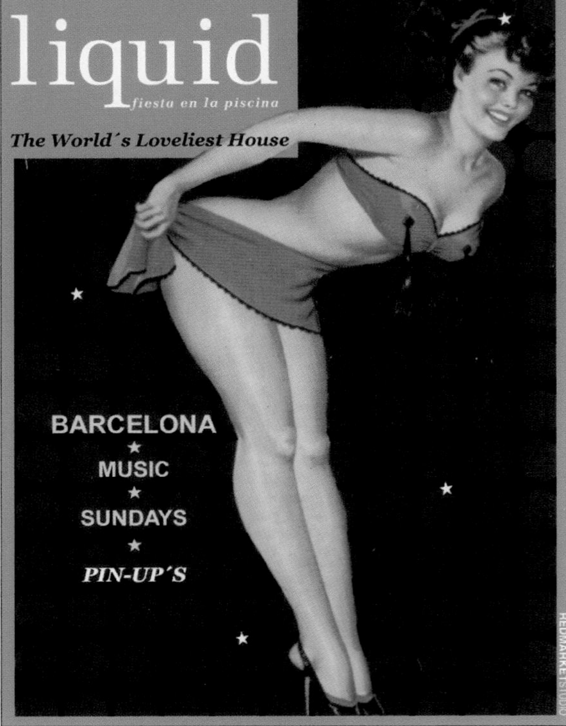

Liquid | Barcelona | Redmarketstudio

Metal Church | Barcelona
Republica | Barcelona
Paradisco @ The Cross | London
Dos Trece | Barcelona
Lokotron | Barcelona | lokotron.com
Risco | Barcelona | nightsungroup.com

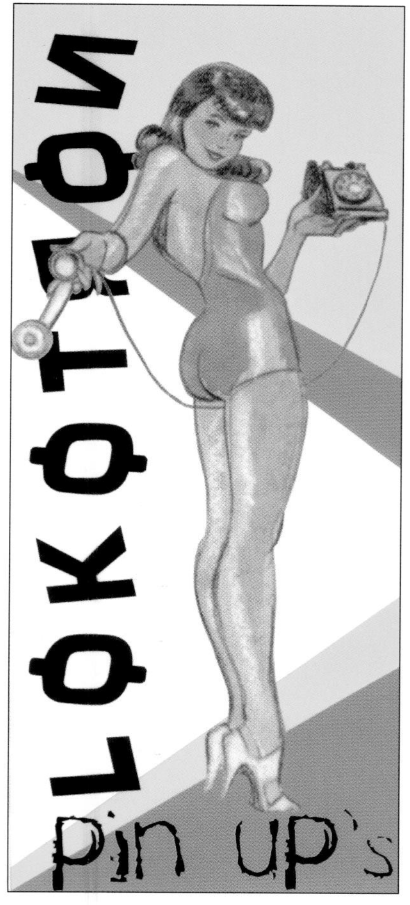

Mond Club I Barcelona I Jordi Labanda + Sergio Ibáñez

MOND CLUB·JULIO DE 2001·CÁNCER

MOND CLUB·AGOSTO DE 2001·LEO

MOND CLUB·SEPTIEMBRE DE 2001·VIRGO

MOND CLUB·OCTUBRE DE 2001·LIBRA

MOND CLUB·ENERO DE 2002·CAPRICORNIO

MOND CLUB·FEBRERO DE 2002·ACUARIO

MOND CLUB·MARZO DE 2002·PISCIS

MOND CLUB·ABRIL DE 2002·ARIES

MOND CLUB·NOVIEMBRE DE 2001·ESCORPIO

MOND CLUB·DICIEMBRE DE 2001·SAGITARIO

MOND CLUB·MAYO DE 2002·TAURO

MOND CLUB·JUNIO DE 2002·GEMINIS

Esta página / This page
Cube Club | Barcelona | Splik
Página derecha / Right page
Plan B. Brixton | London | plan-brixton.co.uk

PLAN B.
BRIXTON.
MARCH 2005
plan
WWW.PLAN-BRIXTON.CO.UK
ACADEMY

Fonfone | Barcelona | Mire & Dave, Wipeoutgraphix

Mascotte | Zurich | Daniel Bolliger
New York Club | Barcelona

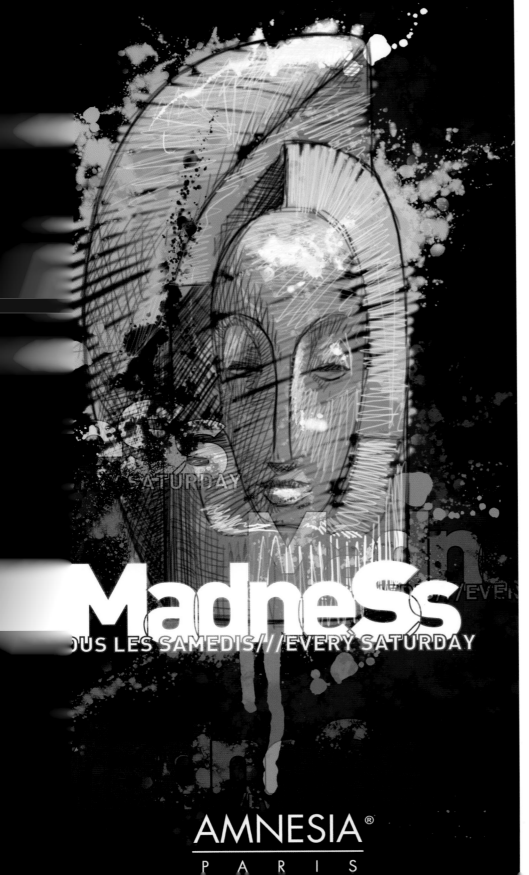

SATURDAY
/EVER
MadneSs
OUS LES SAMEDIS///EVERY SATURDAY
AMNESIA®
PARIS

GURUBCN

GURUBCN

CABARET
UNDERGROUND RIOT!
JULY JULIO 2005
ISSUE 01 $0

Fotos: SCREAMERS
INFO@CABARETLIFE.COM
CABARET
DRESS UP, BE COOL, YOU PUNK! AT
SIDECAR • PLAZA REAL 7 • BARCELONA
01. DJs POST PUNK PRESENT!! CESAR LORES + PETER + NOTCHEFF (MINILIVE)
08. DJs HOSOI (DELOREAN) + CESAR LORES
15. DJs JOAN LUNA (MONDO SONORO) + PETER PUNK
22. DJs BLUE + CESAR LORES
28. DJs VERACRUZ SOUNDSYSTEM + COCO NITZA
EVERY THURSDAY | CADA JUEVES DANCING ROCK!
00.30-4.30 6€ + DRINK
-2€ BEFORE 02.00h !!
Sidecar

CABARET
UNDERGROUND RIOT!
SEPT 2005
ISSUE 03 $0

Fotos: X RAY SPEX
CABARET
SIDECAR • PLAZA REAL 7 • BARCELONA
7. INAUGURACION / OPENNING DJs COCO NITZA + CESAR LORES + PETER PUNK
14. DJs JAIME CAZAS + CESAR LORES
21. DJs AMABLE RAZZAMATAZZ + CESAR LORES
28. DJs GIRLS SPIN THE HITS! + BLUETONIC
EVERY THURSDAY | CADA JUEVES DANCING ROCK!
00.30-4.30 6€ + DRINK
-2€ BEFORE 02.00h !!
Sidecar

Cabaret I Barcelona I LeCadavre
Páginas siguientes / Next pages
Club Catwalk I Barcelona I clubcatwalk.net

GANG S TER
CITY
–NO, hamster NO,
he dicho:
Gangster.
Presenta:
JUEVES / THURSDAY
1, 15 & 29 · JULIO
GANGSTER
CITY

GANG S TER
CITY
587
GANGSTER
CITY
12-8 26-8
JUEVES-THURSDAY

City Loud
Just when you thought the funk couldn't get any funkier, City Loud invites down Junior
summer special. With tracks like E Samba, Thrill Me, Da Hype, Make Luv and Hypnotizing
Joining the boys for their City Loud debut will be our beloved ressie CJ Mackintosh. CJ's
Estonia's Rulers of the Deep, who'll be keeping the backroom jumping with an exclusive 6
Saturday 19th June
Room 1
Junior Jack
Room 2
Tallinn Express
Richard M

En esta página / This page
City Loud | London | Jennie Rushdon + Ed Coward
Derecha / Right page
Zouk club | Singapore | Mriz

two of house music's newest superstars, to turn on the charm at City Loud's
the world over, there simply isn't any escaping these guys at the moment!!
set of the night alongside Birthday girl Lottie, warm up fave Richard M and
nly place to be on Saturday 19th June… stay out late!!
4. Turnmills
& Kid Crème
sh, Lottie
Deep
Special Extended 6 Hour Set
10pm - 6am
63b Clerkenwell Road, London EC1. Tube: Farringdon.
Tel: 020 7250 3409, www.turnmills.co.uk. www.cityloud.com
Limited advanced tickets available now priced at £12 exclusively through:
www.ticketweb.co.uk. Tel: 08700 600 100. £15 otherwise.
Subscribe to our awesome eflyer by emailing: cityloud_subscribe@turnmills.co.uk
TURNMILLS
City Loud
UNDERGROUND
SOUNDS
FOR THE
LOUDEST
KIDS
IN TOWN

Gay Tea Dance | Barcelona | David Cantero

Ilustracion:www.ivansoldo.com

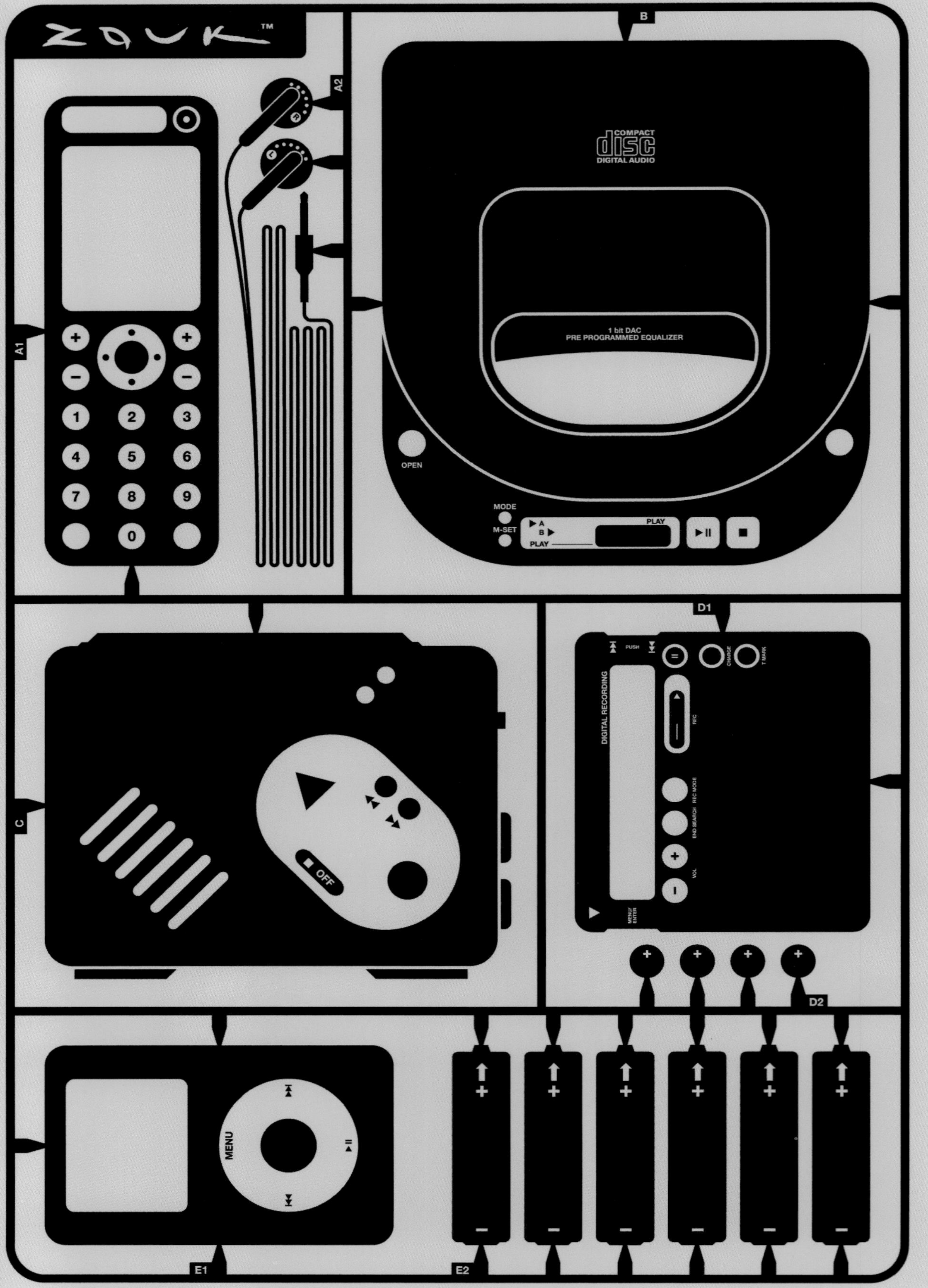

ZOUK™
A1
A2
B
COMPACT disc DIGITAL AUDIO
1 bit DAC
PRE PROGRAMMED EQUALIZER
OPEN
MODE
M-SET
A
B
PLAY
PLAY
1 2 3
4 5 6
7 8 9
0
C
OFF
D1
PUSH
CHARGE
T MARK
DIGITAL RECORDING
REC
REC MODE
END SEARCH
VOL
MENU/ENTER
D2
E1
MENU
E2

En estas páginas / On these pages
Electronic Soccer | Paris | Grégoire Dalle
Zouk Club | Singapore | Jim

Avaland I Hollywood, CA I Stuart Patterson

Avaland | Hollywood, CA | Stuart Patterson

Avalon | New York city | Stuart Patterson

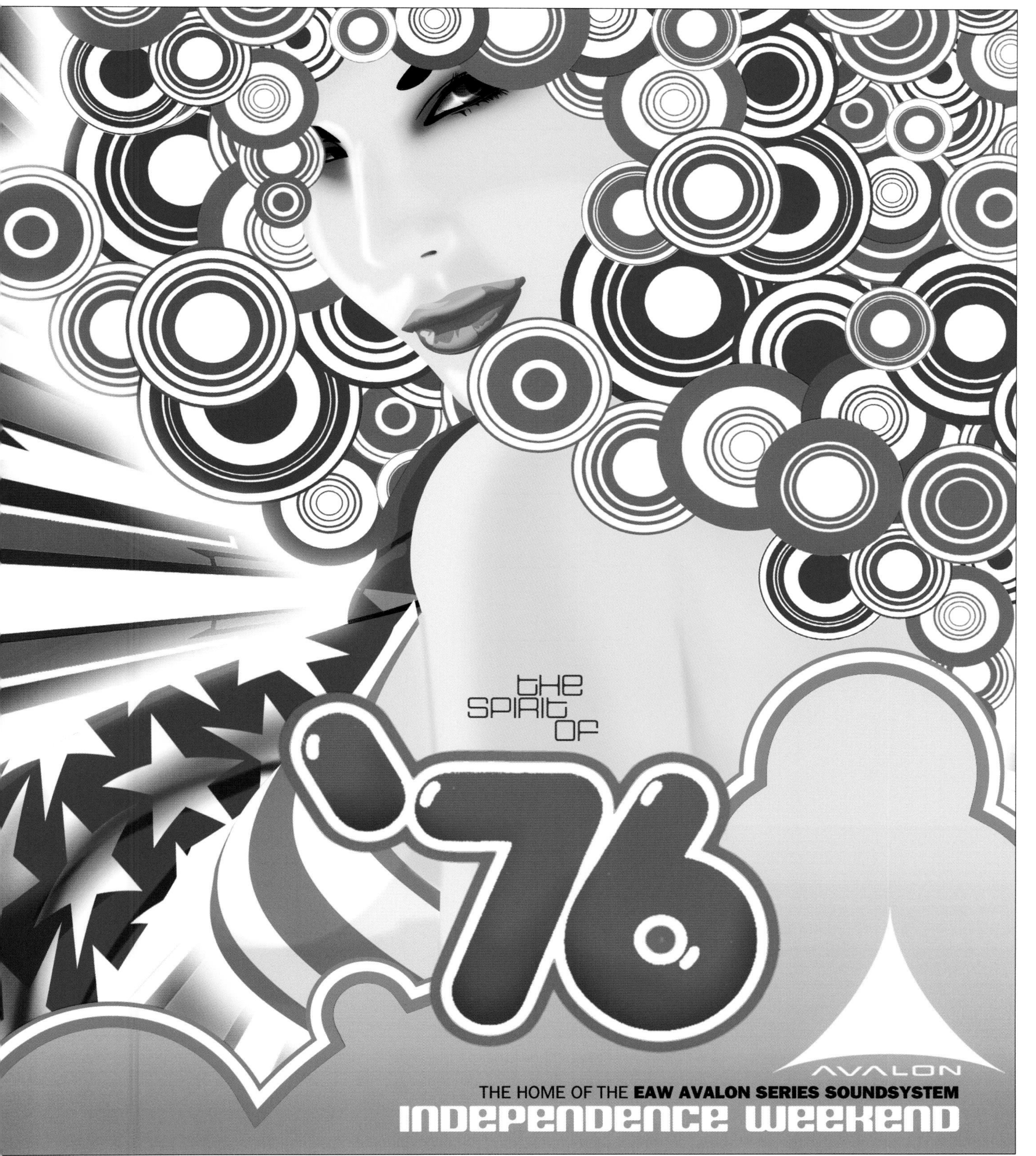
the spirit of
'76
AVALON
THE HOME OF THE EAW AVALON SERIES SOUNDSYSTEM
INDEPENDENCE WEEKEND

FRESH
&
ORGANICALLY
GROWN
IN
avaland
AUGUST 05

SATURDAYS IN AUGUST
MAX GRAHAM & DJ RAP
WAX
ON THE PATIO with
TONY WATSON
08. 06.
doors at 10.30pm
DAVE RALPH
DEMI
KAZELL
FRICTION
ON THE PATIO with
CASEY DESMET
& BRIDGEPORT
08. 13.
doors at 10.30pm
GUS-GUS & KASKADE
STEVE DONOVAN
BASIC
ON THE PATIO with
JOHN DO
& JUSTIN GOURLEY
08. 20.
doors at 10.30pm
BAD BOY BILL
STATIC REVENGER
DAVID MOSES
MEAT KATIE
ON THE PATIO with
the ARCHITECTS OF SOUND
08. 27.
doors at 09.30pm
Avaland.
Saturday Nites at Avalon, Hollywood
1735 N. Vine Street
HOLLYWOOD
advance tickets:
groovetickets.com
graphics by colorola.com
produced by giant · wiredla.com
& avalon hollywood

AVALAND
SATURDAYS
AVALON
1735 N. Vine Street
Hollywood
Saturday. July 2. 2005
Dimitri from Paris with the Idjut Boys
(and helluh more.)
1
Celebrating one year
in Hollywood.
Young enough to party.
Old enough to know how.

En estas páginas / On these pages
Ohm Dance Club | Madrid | Iván Soldo

DANCE
Ilustracion: Ivansoldo.com

i WANT TO
ROCK you
ILUSTRACION:WWW.IVANSOLDO.COM

DISCO
KING
ohm
dance club
ilustracion:www.ivansoldo.com
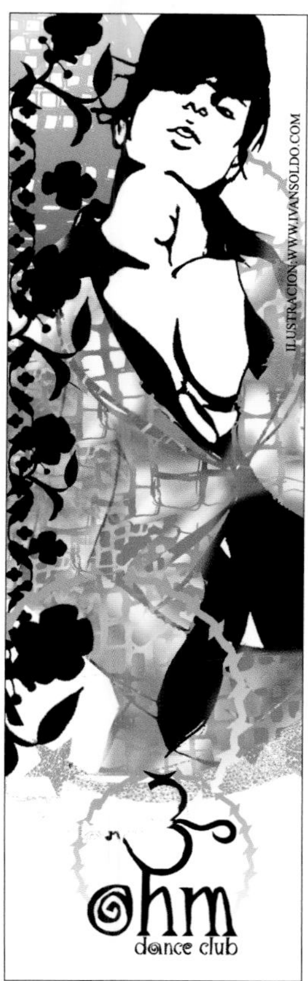
ILUSTRACION:WWW.IVANSOLDO.COM
ohm
dance club

WWW.IVANSOLDO.COM

Ilustracion:www.ivansoldo.com

ILUSTRACION:WWW.IVANSOLDO.COM

En estas páginas / On these pages
Dirty Dancing I Brussels I Luis Arenas

Sky funk

En estas páginas / On these pages
Club Catwalk I Barcelona I Oscar Cardó

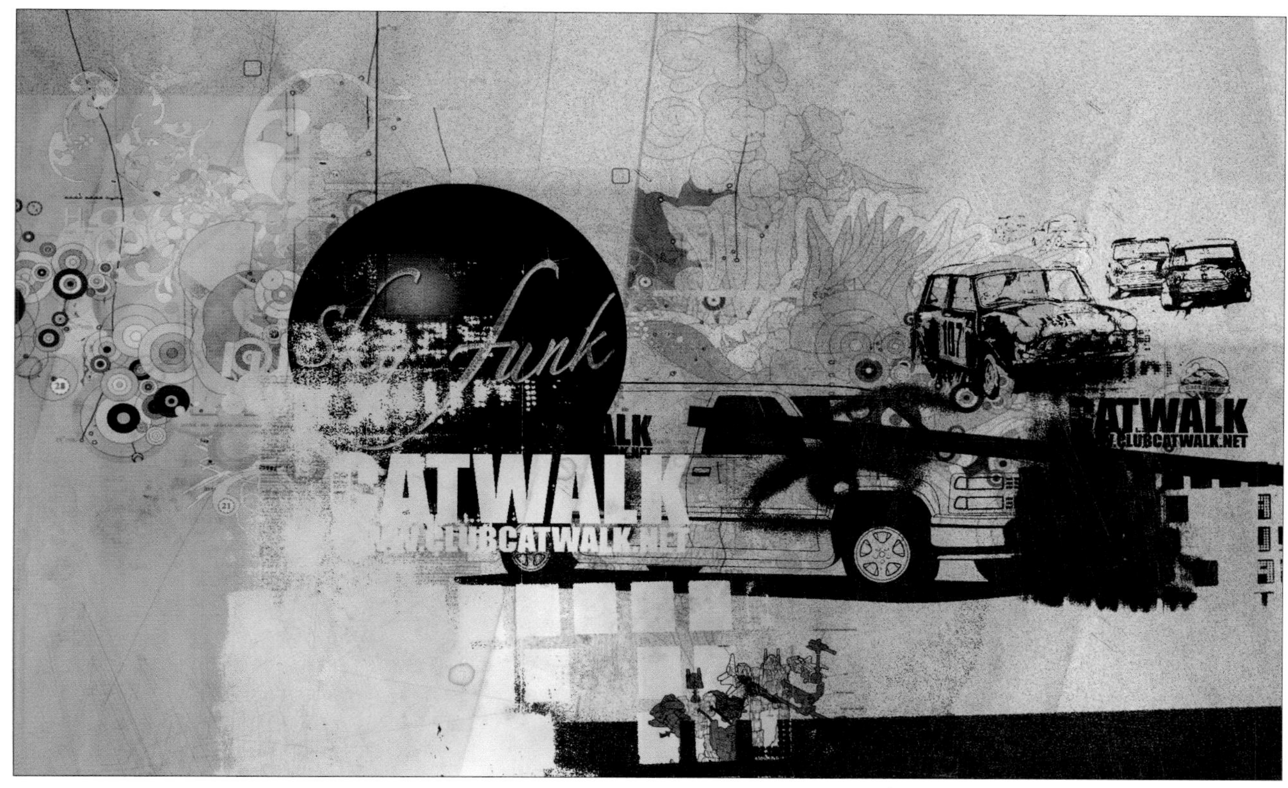

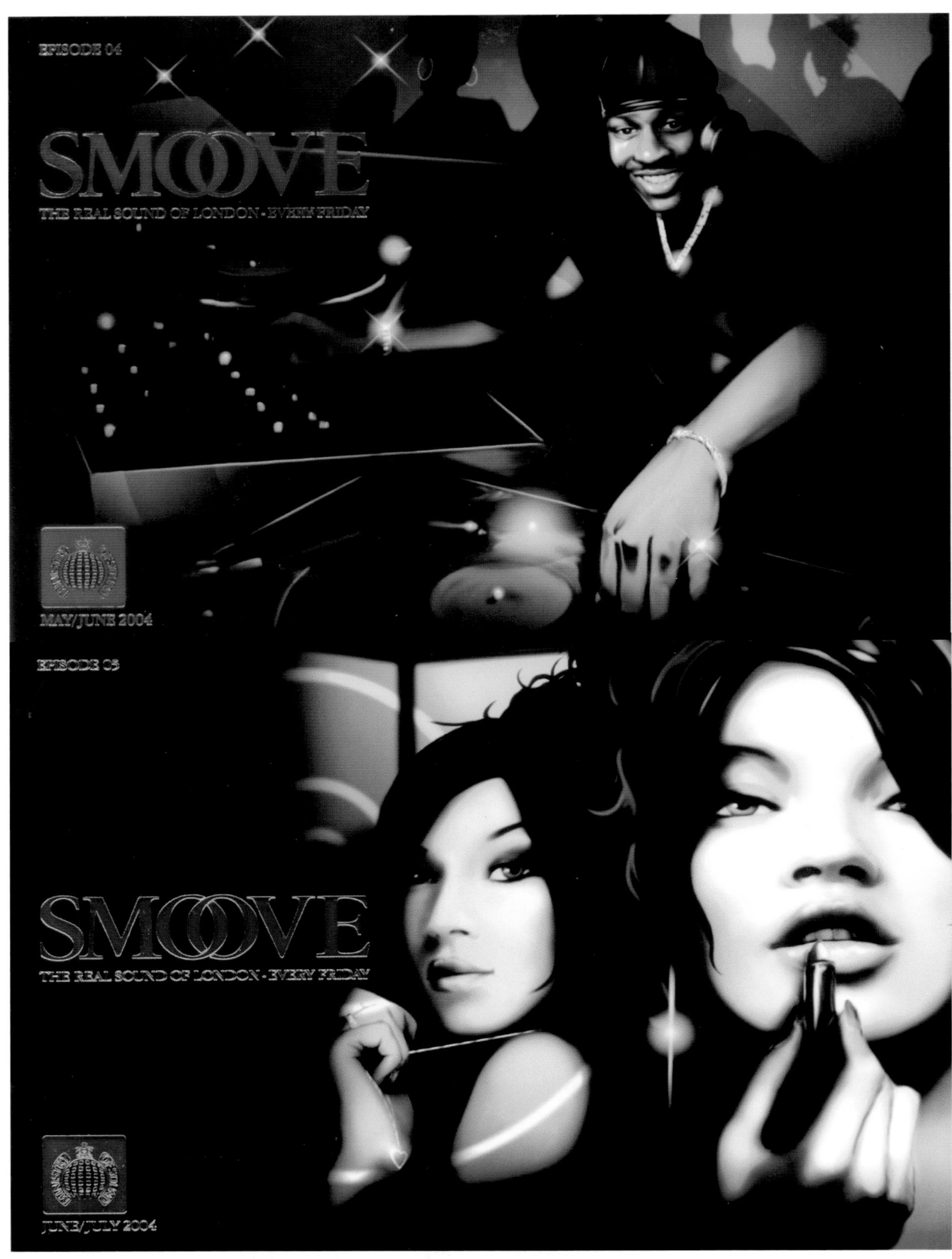

Ministry of Sound | London | AMP Associates & Rob Cheetham

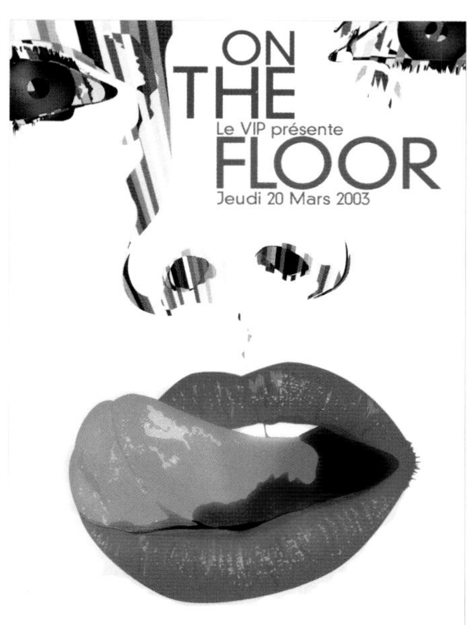

High west city | London
Club Danzatoria | Barcelona
Le Vip | Paris | The Flyer Designers
Catwalk | Barcelona | Oscar Cardó

333 Saturdays March Listings

333 Saturdays
January Listings
All events at
333 Old Street
London EC1V 9LE
10.00pm-5.00am £5 b4 11/ £10/ £8 NUS/members
Info: 0207 729 4223 www.off-centre.com
Buy cheaper tickets online at www.ticketweb.co.uk.
Bypass the queue, get cheaper tickets and guarantee yourself entry by booking online.
Tickets are on sale now at £8 instead of £10.
Visit www.off-centre.com for up to the minute info, DJ top tens & exclusive competitions
Visit www.333mother.com for all 333 listings.
333
sat

En estas páginas / On these pages
333 Saturdays I London I Elliot Thoburn
Página siguiente / Next page
Shôko I Barcelona I Oscar Cardó

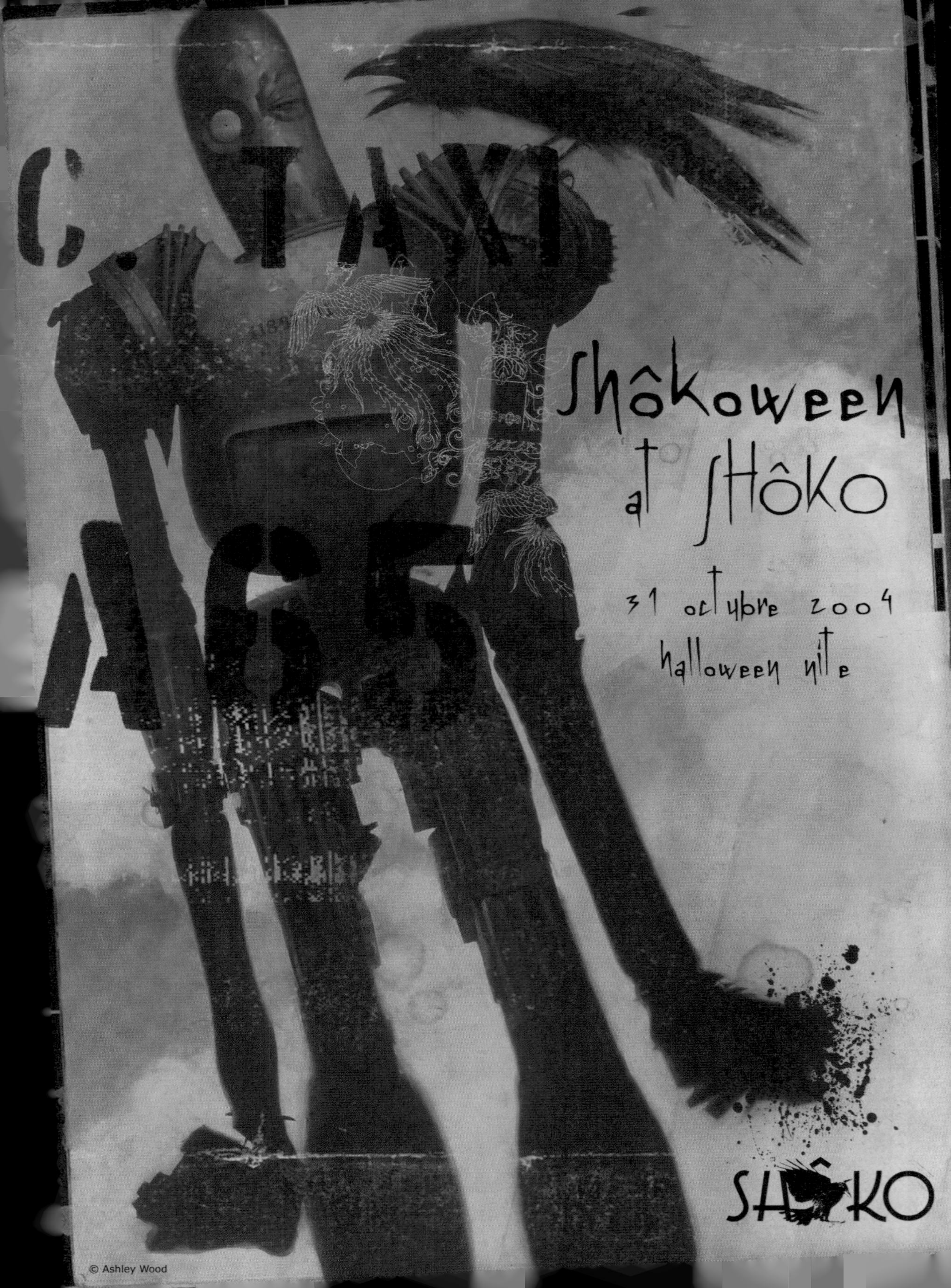

Shôkoween

at Shôko

31 octubre 2004

halloween nite

SHÔKO

31 octubre 2004

halloween nite

Shôkoween at Shôko

OKI OKI YOU MUST HAVE HEARD OF MADAM BAT! FUCK, DUDE, WHERE WAS YOUR HEAD AT? THIS STUFF WAS WORLD NEWS! MADAM BAT? YOU KNOW, HER FAMOUS VAMPIRE STAG MOVIES? EVERYONE THOUGHT THE VAMPIRE THING WAS ALL AN ACT. REAL DEAL, BABY! MY DAD GOT TO KNOW HER REAL WELL – SHE'S MY MOTHER. PRETTY COOL, EH? STILL DIDN'T STOP DAD FROM ICING HER JUST AFTER SHE GAVE BIRTH. MMM. ALLWAYS GETS ME. COLD MAN, MY FATHER – COLD.

madam bat

SO, FAMOUS MONSTER HUNTER. COOL VAMPIRE SHAGGING/KILLING MACHINE, HE HAS THE WORLD AT HIS FEET...

the thought of my death never leaves me

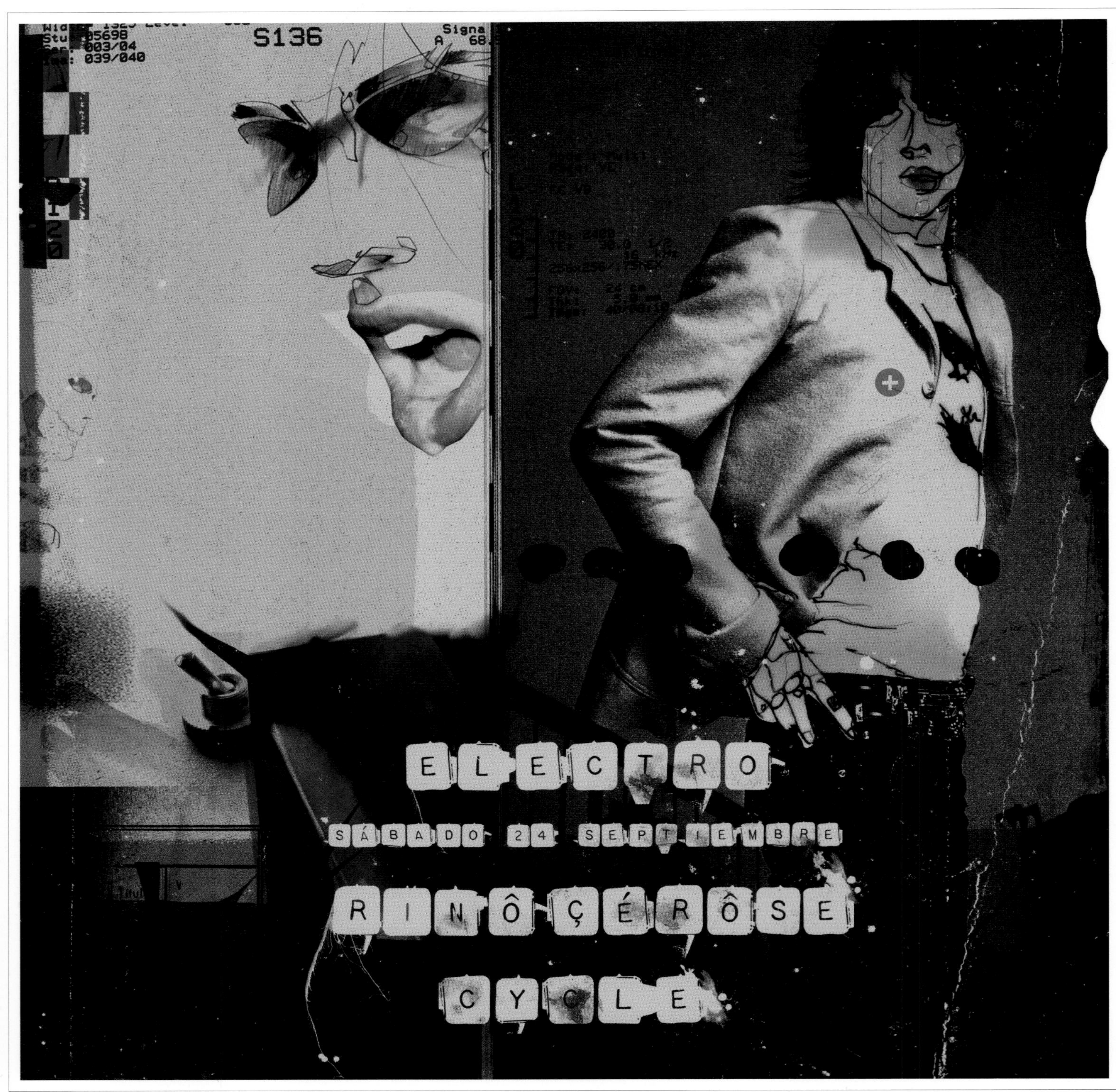

Mtv España I Barcelona I Oscar Cardó

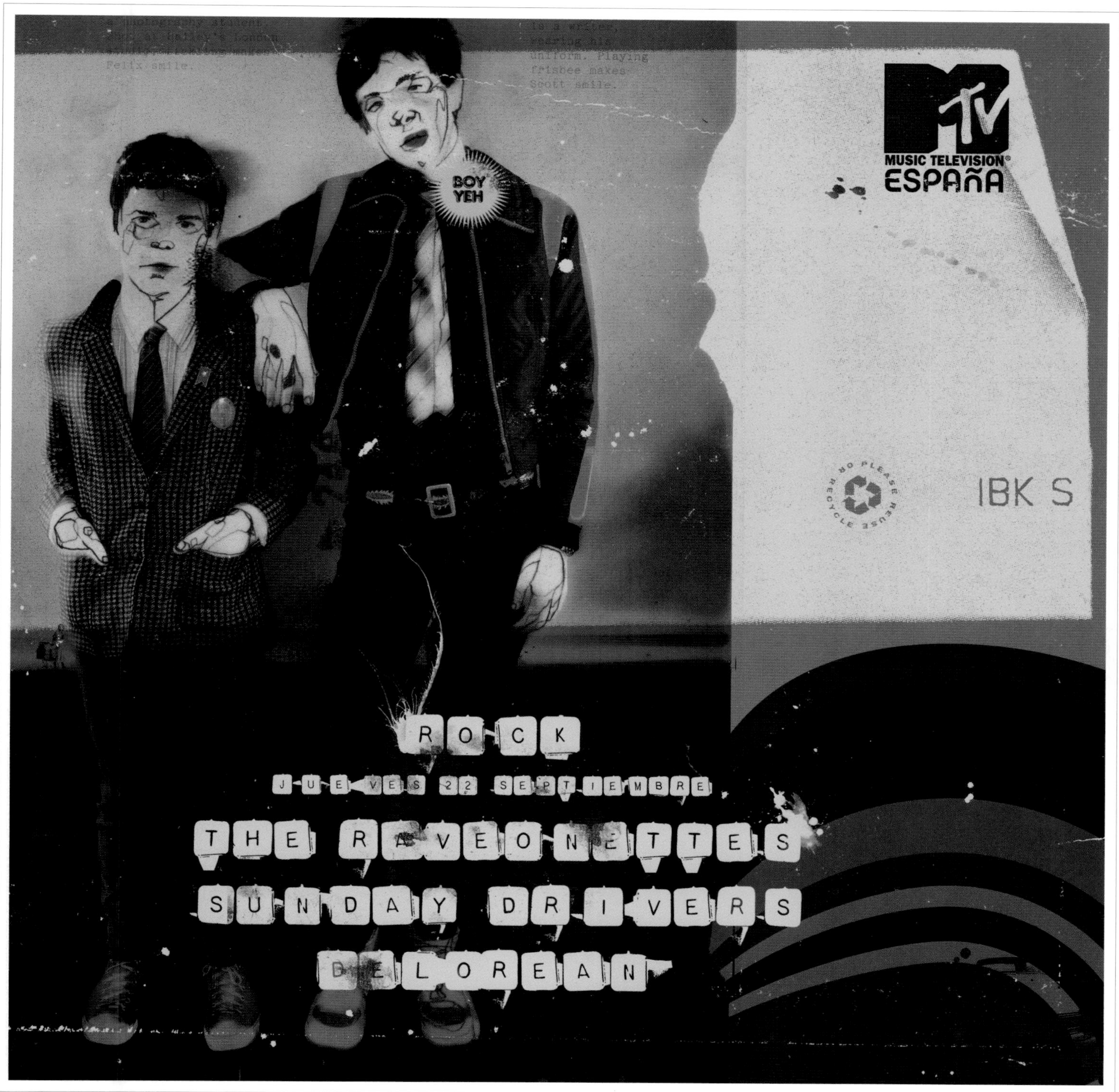

Mtv España | Barcelona | Oscar Cardó

En esta página / This page
Lady Miss Kier party | Los Angeles | Eduardo Souza
Unique Club | Düserldorff | Frank Popp
Dirty Dancing | Belgium | Luis Arenas
Siroco | Madrid | Chop
Página derecha / Right page
Wigstock Festival | New York City | Scott Lifshutz

SIROCO
C/San Dimas 3
www.siroco.es

00:30h.
Sábado 12 de Junio
Miss Kier dj.
Deee-Lite

00:30h.
Sabado 12 de Junio
MISS KIER dj. JJ BERNARDO - GUDLAK

Siroco tiene el placer de presentar en primicia para Madrid a Kier Kirby más conocida como Lady Miss Kier, mítica vocalista, co-productora y bailarina de los no menos miticos Deee Lite. Su primer single "Groove Is In The Heart", editado en el 91, que pasó de ser un white label para dj's a vender millones de copias, significaba un equilibrio perfecto entre Las demandas del mercado pop y las necesidades de las pistas de baile, resumiendo el hedonismo químico De aquella época. En el 95 se traslado a Londres y empezó a ejercer de Dj, recorriendo el planeta con su maleta de discos cargada de groove para ofrecer sets que fusionan distintos estilos de lo que ella misma llama "future funk" y que oscilan entre Breaks, electro, funk y house.

00:30h.
Viernes 25 de Junio
TIM "LOVE" LEE (TUMMY TOUCH RECORDS)

Y el último viernes del mes tendremos la presencia tras los platos de nuestra cabina a uno de los personajes más carismáticos de la escena de baile: nada más y nada menos que a TIM "LOVE" LEE el "capo" del sello Tummy Touch (descubridores de Groove Armada). Ha publicado ya tres discos, un sin fin de remezclas para artistas consagrados, así como una recopilación a modo de sesión ("It's all good"). Tim "Love" Lee ya nos visitó hace dos años y todos los que vivimos la experiencia, la recordamos como algo inolvidable: una sesión repleta de buen rollo, eclecticismo musical en donde puso de todo ("hip-hop beats", electro-breaks & "dirty house like grooves"), y excelente comunicación entre el dj y todos los que allí moviamos el culo... SI PUEDES, NO TE LO PIERDAS... para paladares exquisitos.

Mas información en www.siroco.es

Diseño: chop

WiGSTOCK 98
Sunday
Sept.6th
1998
2pm-10:30pm
Pier 54 at 13th St.
& West Side Highway
in the West Village, NYC
Benefiting GMHC &
Beautycares
$15 / $20 at the door, if available
Tickets availabe at:
West Village
Lips, Patricia Field, P. Chanin's Loft
Chelsea
P. Chanin
Raymond Dragon
or by Phone at 800-494-TIXS
presented by
Virgin
MEGASTORE
MUSIC MOVIES BOOKS SOFTWARE
and
Virgin Cola
Burp!
michael
economy
HX FOR HER
NEW YORK CITY
HX MAGAZINE
NEW YORK CITY
NAYA
flamingo
east

WIGSTOCK
LABOR DAY
NOON TIL SIX
AT THOMPKINS SQUARE PARK
SEPT 1
3 TEENS KILL 4
ETHYL EICHELBERGER ✻ JOHN SEX ✻ DEAN JOHNSON
EFFERSON HAIRPLANE ✻ TABBOO ✻ MING VAUZE
SISTER DIMENSION ✻ KENNON RAINES
ANGELLA DEVILLE ✻ AUDREY WHITE ✻ HAPI PHACE
TALL LONESOME PINES ✻ STEPHANIE CRAWFORD
DAINTY ADORE O'HARA ✻ KATHY HARWOOD
PETER KWALOFF AS DIANNE MARKOWITZ
JOHN EPPERSON ✻ AND SOME SPECIAL SURPRISES!
HOSTESSED BY THE LADY BUNNY
WITH THE WIGSTOCK ENSEMBLE

WIGSTOCK 89

WIGSTOCK '91
IN ASSOCIATION WITH
CROW BAR * CREATIVE TIME * LIMELIGHT * COFFEE SHOP
step lightly girls!
remember - flats are in
please respect the lawn
all welcome... except litterbugs
LABOR DAY MONDAY SEP. 2 12pm - 8pm
raindate Sunday, Sep. 8
UNION SQUARE PARK (Broadway & 14th St.)

WIGSTOCK'92
HAIR
PEACE
LABOR DAY - MONDAY SEPT. 7 from 12 - 8 pm
TOMPKINS SQUARE PARK
sponsored by: MAC, NAYA & Limelight
(raindate Sat. Sept.12)

WIGSTOCK BENEFIT!
Join The "Lady" Bunny and Manhattan's zaniest superstars as we turn the Pyramid out once again at this dynamite foot-stompin' extravaganza to benefit a bankrupt Wigstock '92
featuring!
John Kelly
Sister Dimension
Lahoma van Zandt
Barbara Patterson Lloyd
Flotilla Debarge
nonsense
Wear your DIAPERS 'cuz this show's gonna PEE!
dj Tennessee
whores
Ru-Paul
Joey Arias
Endive
Freda
all kindsa shit!
boozin'
retards
videos
comedy
Tuesday August 4 $6
at the PYRAMID 101 Ave. A
performance at midnight
11:30 downstairs screening of Tom Rubnitz's Wigstock the Movie

The "Lady" Bunny
wigstock '94
10th anniversary
Noon to Nine Rain or Shine
Sensible Shoes Always Suggested
Labor Day Weekend
Sunday September 4, 1994
The Piers at Christopher & West Street
With these Wacked-Out Performers:
Barbara Patterson Lloyd
Barbara Tucker
Bertha
Crystal Waters
Daphne
Debbie Harry
Deeaundra Peek
Drag-In
Duelling Bankheads
Ebony Jett
Ffloyd
Girlina
Hedda Lettuce
India
Joey Arias
JoJo Americo & Miss Guy
Lahoma van Zandt
Linda Simpson
Lurleen Wallace
Matthew Kasten's boy bar Beauties featuring Toddrique, Afrodite, Babe Duke, Sweetie, Randella, Flotilla DeBarge, Miss Missy, Candis Cayne, Raven Oh
Michael West
Miss Coco Peru
Miss Understood
Misstress Formika
Mona Foote
Morph
Pat
Raga Mountain Woman
RuPaul
Ryan Laundry
Satellite Dish
Sherry Vine
Tabboo!
Tartar
Ultra Nate'
Varla Jean Merman
Wendy Wild
The Wigstock Dancers with Vanier, Serena Dubois, Candis Cayne, Girlina, and Miss Honey Dijon
and your emcee
The "Lady" Bunny
OFFICIAL Wigstock After Party/Benefit at
USA
218 West 47th Street
starts at 10pm $10 with
HX
MAC
flamingo east
NAYA
JOSE CUERVO
out

WIGSTOCK 99
SUNDAY SEPTEMBER 5TH
Pier 54 • 2 pm until 10:30 pm
Proceeds benefit Gay Men's Health Crisis
$15 in advance/$20 at the door • 1-800-494-TIXS
THE BIG TEASE
genre
NAYA

WIGSTOCK 2000
sunday sept. 3
2-10pm
pier 54
14th St. & west side hwy
tkts available at:
Lips, P. Chanin, P. Chanin's Loft, Patricia Field & Raymond Dragon
or call
boxoffice tickets.com
800 494 TIXS • 877 TDD TIXS
$15 advance/$20 day of
www.wigstock.nu
hotline: 212-439-5139
genre
HX
VOICE
BACARDI
GMHC

WIGSTOCK 97
Presented by
MAC
A Benefit for Beauty Cares, Beauty Industry for AIDS Care & Gay Men's Health Crisi
NAYA
Webster Hall

Get ready to flip your wig with The "Lady" Bunny & a cast of thousands
SUNDAY SEPT. 3
1-10PM
The Piers at Christopher & West Streets
rain or shine
WIGSTOCK
NAYA
MAC
crowbar

wigstock 2004
on
saturday
august 21st
5:00-7:00pm
at
tompkins square park
presented by:
HOWL!
2nd ANNUAL FESTIVAL OF EAST VILLAGE ARTS

wigstock
AUG. 23
BACK TO ITS ROOTS
4:30-6:30PM TOMPKINS SQUARE PARK, EAST VILLAGE
THIS WIGSTOCK SPECIAL EDITION POSTER BROUGHT TO YOU BY BORU VODKA.
HTTP://WWW.HOWLFESTIVAL.COM - HTTP://WWW.BORUVODKA.US
BORU VODKA

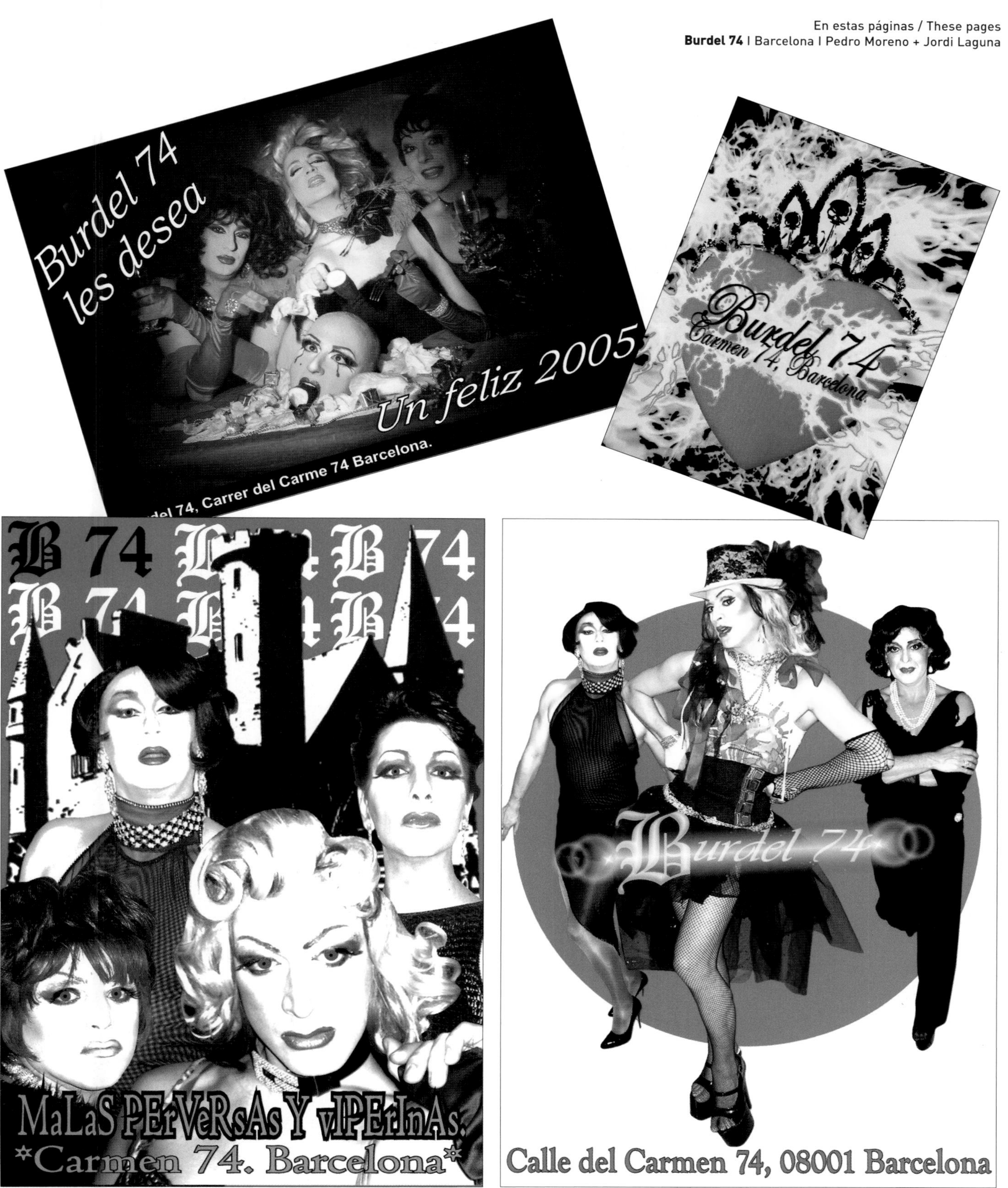
Burdel 74
les desea
Un feliz 2005
del 74, Carrer del Carme 74 Barcelona.
Burdel 74
Carmen 74, Barcelona
B 74 B 74 B 74
B 74 B 74 B 74
MaLaS PErVeRsAs Y vIPErInAs.
Carmen 74. Barcelona
Burdel 74
Calle del Carmen 74, 08001 Barcelona

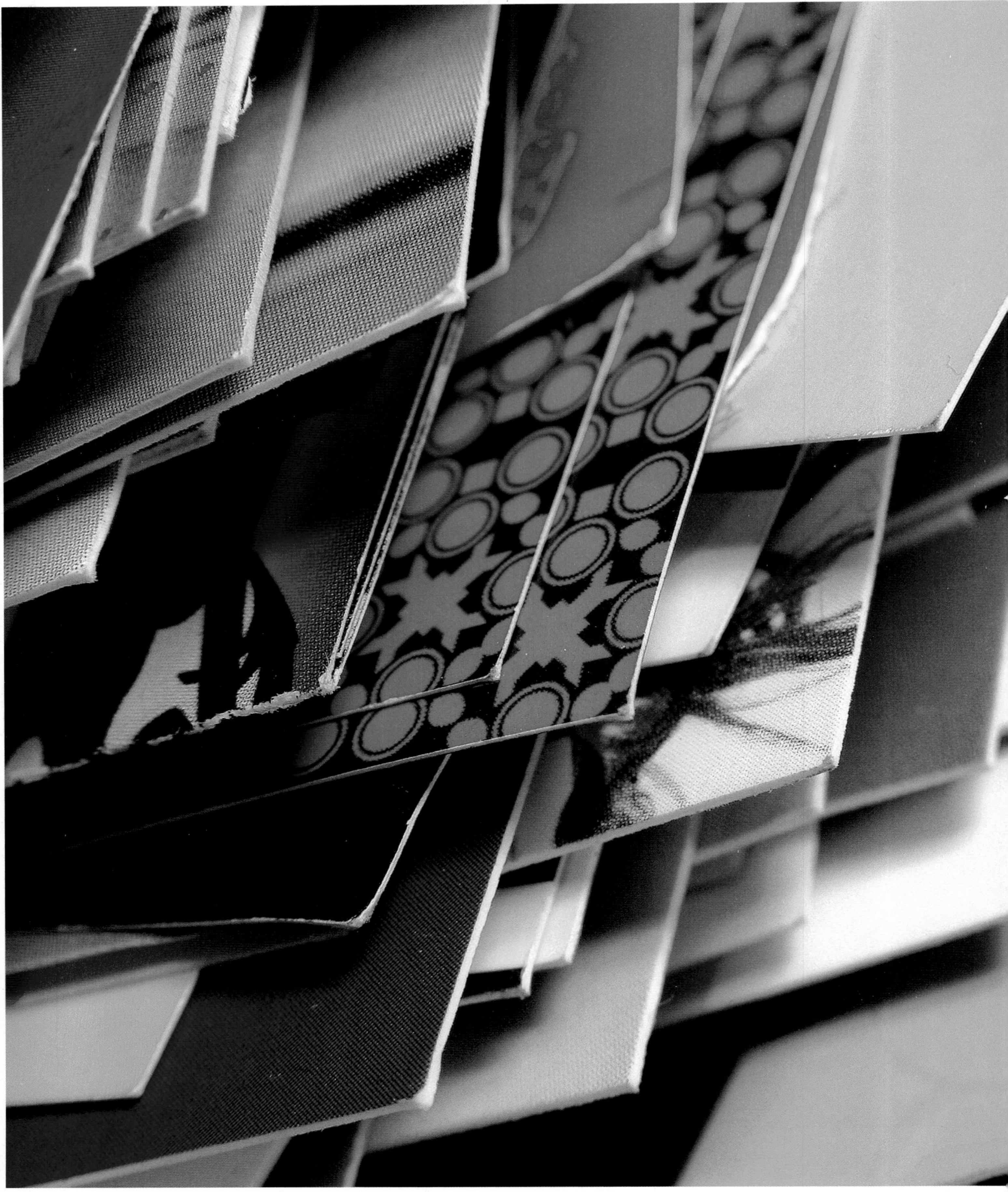